LONDON'S LABYRINTH

THE WORLD BENEATH THE CITY'S STREETS

LONDON'S LABYRINTH

THE WORLD BENEATH THE CITY'S STREETS

FIONA RULE

Ian Allan PUBLISHING

First published 2012

ISBN 9780711035447

Published by Ian Allan Publishing
An imprint of Ian Allan Publishing Ltd, Hersham, Surrey KT12 4RG

Printed and bound by CPI Group (UK) Ltd, Croydon, CR0 4YY

Visit the Ian Allan website at www.ianallanpublishing.com

CONTENTS

For Mum – the person with whom I first ventured into
London's Labyrinth, via the Piccadilly Line.

ACKNOWLEDGEMENTS

I would like to thank the immensely knowledgeable and helpful staff at the London Transport Museum, the National Archives, the Westminster Archives and the London Metropolitan Archives for their assistance with my research.

I am also indebted to Celia Harrison, Jack Hawkins and Akile Osman at London Underground for their generous assistance and would like to express my gratitude for the help that the late Suki Harrison gave me by putting me in touch with these knowledgeable people.

Finally, many thanks to my agent, Sheila Ableman, for her advice and guidance, Nick Grant and Paul Woods at Ian Allan Publishing, for their faith in me as a writer and, last but not least, my husband Robert for his constant support.

INTRODUCTION

My journey into London's underground labyrinth began on a warm July afternoon, in the leafy communal gardens that lay behind the redbrick walls of a mansion block in west London. A residents' party was in full swing and, as the wine flowed and tempting smells wafted from the barbecue, I struck up a conversation with a fellow partygoer. I told her about my fascination with London, and how I'd always been especially interested in the city hidden beneath our feet. 'There's all sorts of things down there,' I enthused. 'Old tunnels, bunkers, disused Tube stations ...'

'My daughter works for London Underground,' she told me. 'She might be able to show you around some of those abandoned stations.' So began my exploration of the secrets of subterranean London.

London's underground railway is indeed a labyrinth. Although hundreds of its winding tunnels are seen by thousands of travellers every day, there are many more that lie dark and deserted beneath the city streets, hidden from view behind anonymous doors, ignored by hordes of commuters who pass them every day. But, for anyone interested in the history of the city, these blank doors are the gateway into a wonderland.

On a quiet street off Piccadilly, a graffiti-covered entrance leads to a tiny stairwell that descends into total blackness. This is what remains of Down Street Tube station, an abandoned stop on the Piccadilly Line. Never having been used very much, the station closed its doors in 1932 – only to find an unlikely purpose as a secret government bunker known as 'the Burrow', during World War 2.

Soon after the grave declaration of war was made, Down Street's abandoned platforms were hurriedly bricked up and the station became the makeshift headquarters of the Emergency Railway Committee, whose unenviable task was to keep London moving throughout the duration of the conflict. Their subterranean headquarters served them so well that Winston Churchill and his cabinet used some of the rooms from time to time. As Hitler's bombs began to rain down on the city, soberly dressed civil servants, cabinet members, secretaries and telephonists slipped quietly through the station's side door and made the way down to their top-secret workplace. Here they would stay for hours, or sometimes days, at a time, concealed from the view of passengers on the trains rushing past the platform's edge.

Today, the Down Street war bunker is long deserted but its shell still remains, along with a few clues to its incongruous former use. In a narrow, claustrophobic corridor an old telephone switchboard stands in the darkness, covered with 60 years of dust and grime. Other, smaller rooms in the complex are still fitted with washing facilities, for staff forced to sleep there when the Blitz was at its most ferocious.

My exploration of the underground railway's hidden places revealed the many diverse stories the Tube network has to tell. At Aldgate, I was shown the shadowy remains of the original station, just visible in the fading light before blackness engulfs the tunnel. At Moorgate, the tiny blind tunnel that a packed Northern Line train ploughed into at full speed, one terrible day in 1975, was grimly indicated. The front carriage of the doomed train slammed into the tunnel wall with such force that the two carriages immediately behind it were forced up and under each other, trapping the people inside in a tangled forest of warped metal and shattered glass. The scene that met the men and women who came to rescue them must have been hellish.

I found my excursions underground fascinating, sometimes unnerving but always intriguing. The stories I uncovered inspired me to journey deeper into the subterranean city, to explore all the facets of this complex labyrinth. What I found was a hidden network as essential to the life of London as anything above ground. From the miles of electrical and telecom cabling secreted beneath the pavements to the sewers that carry the city's waste, what goes on beneath London is essential to the city's existence.

Underground London is largely Victorian. Britain's emergence as a 19th-century superpower prompted its capital to grow at an alarmingly fast rate. Suddenly, the above-ground infrastructure that had worked for centuries became woefully insufficient. Faced with such a challenge, Victorian engineers found the answer lay beneath their feet. Thus the underground labyrinth began to evolve, in order to enable London to survive.

The fetid miasmas created by the 'Great Stink' of 1858 prompted the engineer Joseph Bazalgette to originate one of London's first underground innovations – a network of subterranean pipes that carried away the city's rotting detritus.

This visionary project saved countless Londoners from the horrors of the deadly water-borne disease that had ravaged the city for generations.

The first forays beneath the streets were dirty and massively disruptive, as teams of burly 'navvies' dug colossal trenches into which pipes and tunnels were laid. As Londoners picked their way through the towering piles of earth that lined the streets, a man named James Greathead was busy putting the finishing touches to his 'tunnelling shield' – a monstrously large circular device that worked on similar lines to a giant pastry cutter, slicing through the sticky subterranean clay and avoiding the need to start digging above ground. The 'Greathead Shield', as it became known, took the subterranean city into a new era where no project was deemed impossible. Soon, the labyrinth beneath the streets began to stretch away from the city centre, toward the new housing estates that lay on its perimeter, providing the residents with water, light and transport – with all workings hidden from view.

Since then, the city under London has found other, more ominous uses. Ministers and military men followed the course of World War 2 from bunkers buried deep beneath the streets, while civilians sat anxiously in subterranean shelters and deep-level Tube stations, listening to Hitler's bombs raining down on the city above. Later, the Cold War prompted the construction of ever deeper shelters that might give a handful of Londoners a chance of surviving the atom bomb.

Today, parts of London's bafflingly complex network of underground tunnels and pipelines are over a hundred years old. The labyrinth has acquired its own history and folklore. Fascinating stories abound of abandoned tunnels, ghost stations and shadowy spaces hidden beneath the city streets.

Over the last two centuries, subterranean London has continued to grow and evolve. Today, its labyrinthine byways stretch out for miles, from the centre into the adjacent suburbs and surrounding countryside. They are the roots of the city, giving life to the metropolis above.

CHAPTER 1

THE GREAT STINK

The earliest days of June 1858 brought balmy summer weather to London. The city basked under clear skies, interrupted only by occasional brief night-time thunderstorms. However, as mid-month approached, the weather suddenly turned more sultry and oppressive. Temperatures soared to well over 80° Fahrenheit and, as Londoners went about their business along the sun-baked city streets, those closest to the Thames began to notice how the great river's waters were becoming somehow thicker, darker and distinctly fouler smelling.

On Saturday 12 June, a young man who set out from Westminster pier in a small rowing boat, destined for the Crabtree Inn at Putney Reach, was so overcome by the foul-smelling river he was almost compelled to turn back. Further east, lightermen delivering cargo to the tall sailing ships berthed at the docks found the stench so bad in places that they were forced to rush to the side of their boats, where they became repeatedly and violently sick.

As the heat-wave continued unabated, the whole city surrounding the Thames became shrouded in a stinking miasma. Work became almost impossible as Londoners deliberated over which was the lesser of two evils – the heat or the smell. 'T.S.', a lawyer whose offices were in the Temple, wrote, 'The stench … today is sickening and nauseous in the extreme … If I open my windows in rushes the stench; if I close them the heat is so great that I am almost suffocated.'

The lawyer's dilemma was shared by thousands of other Londoners, including Members of Parliament whose meeting rooms at the Palace of Westminster overlooked the river. As temperatures reached a stifling 93° on Wednesday 16 June, MPs at the House of Commons reeled from the stench permeating the rooms closest to the river. *The Times* reported, 'A few members, indeed, bent upon investigating the subject at its very depth, ventured into the library, but they were instantaneously driven to retreat, each man with a handkerchief to his nose.'

Determined to seek out and identify the cause, Parliament's 'Inspector for Ventilation', Mr Goldsworthy Gurney, was dispatched in a boat to investigate the situation on the Thames. During his unpleasant journey, Gurney noticed that the cloudy, reeking water stretched along the entire central section of the river, from Woolwich in the east to Putney in the west. He also saw that this foul-smelling soup primarily comprised sewage. In his subsequent report to the House of Commons, Gurney concluded, 'The water that comes into the Thames no doubt goes to the sea and carries some of the sewage with it, but a very large proportion still remains sufficient to settle on the banks of the river and to produce a nuisance. The black water is deposited on the flats or banks on the sides nearly the whole way.'

The fact that the city's sewage was disgorged into the Thames had been a cause for concern for years. However, the stinking fumes from the river had been at their worst while Parliament was on its summer recess and, consequently, very little had been done to address the problem. The fact that the government was now experiencing the disgusting odour at first hand was wholeheartedly welcomed by the press. On 18 June *The Times* wrote, 'We are heartily glad of it … It is their fault that the river Thames has not … been purified … On Wednesday, when the heat was overpowering, they began to imagine that there was something in the popular outcry. Conviction rose with the quicksilver of the thermometer.'

During the early decades of the 19th century, it had been a popularly held belief that although the odour periodically emanating from the Thames was hugely unpleasant, it was in no way harmful. However, in the 1850s opinion began to change and many London doctors were increasingly concerned that the water may indeed have been carrying a hazard to health.

During the Great Stink of 1858, Bermondsey's chief medical officer, Dr John Challice, wrote, 'I have daily persons consulting me who have been seized with nausea, sickness and diarrhoea, by them attributed to the effects of the effluvia from the river. Some have complained that the peculiar taste remained on their palate for days.' William Ord, surgical registrar of St Thomas's Hospital, investigated the effects of the stench on river workers and noted, 'They described themselves as experiencing, at first languor, and soon afterwards, nausea and pain, beginning most commonly at the temples and spreading over the head. After a time followed giddiness, and in many of them temporary loss or impairment of sight, the presence of black spots before their eyes and often utter mental confusion … In a considerable number the throat was swollen and red, causing much "soreness" and intense thirst.'

The river workers struggled through the physical discomforts caused by its dirty waters, totally unaware that they had fallen prey to one of the most dangerous diseases of the 19th century – cholera.

London experienced its first cholera epidemic in 1832. By the end of that year, it had killed over 6,000 inhabitants. A second epidemic broke out in 1848, killing around 14,000, and the disease would strike again just four years later. As more and more people succumbed to the sickness, a physician named John Snow vowed to stop it in its tracks by proving his theory that cholera was not caused by bad smells – as most people believed – but by contaminated water. He identified a small area of Soho, between Regent Street and Wardour Street, which had been badly affected by the epidemic and questioned local residents about where they obtained their water. To his excitement, a huge proportion of households affected by the disease used a specific pump in Broad Street (today's Broadwick Street). Snow petitioned the local parish council and, after telling them of his findings, persuaded them to remove the pump handle to stop anyone accessing the contents of the well beneath. Once this had been done, the cholera outbreak began to subside.

With the cause now identified, Dr Snow analysed the pump water and investigated the condition of the well. Although the samples yielded nothing conclusive, he was intrigued to discover how the well was situated very close to an old, leaky cesspit. It suddenly became clear that cholera epidemics were not only waterborne but were effectively created by contaminated sewage. Armed with this new information, he turned his attentions to the greatest water source in London – the Thames. His most significant realisation was that riverside companies were systematically poisoning their customers by supplying them with disease-ridden water.

John Snow's discoveries were among the most important scientific advances of the era. However, like many trailblazers before him, he failed to convince the government. His detractors argued that he relied too heavily on circumstantial evidence rather than scientific fact, and further, that by the time the pump handle in Broad Street had been removed, the cholera epidemic was already in decline. This, coupled with the prohibitive expense that a countrywide investigation into levels of water pollution would entail, prompted the authorities to disregard Dr Snow's hypothesis.

Although Snow was largely ignored by those in power, ordinary Londoners were not surprised by his findings. For decades, people living close to the Thames had found its water so unpalatable that they opted to give their children beer, or even gin, to drink. In his book *Town Swamps and Social Bridges*, published a year after the Great Stink, the writer George Godwin noted, 'Fifteen or sixteen years ago, the Thames water was not so bad, and persons on the river did not hesitate at dipping in a vessel and drinking the contents. Such a thing now would be an act of insanity; and yet we are told, on good authority, that in a part of Rotherhithe a number of poor persons, who have no proper water supply, are obliged to use, for drinking and other purposes, the Thames water in its present abominable condition, unfiltered.'

It seems incredible now that London, then the richest and most influential city in the world, had allowed the river at its heart to become so horrendously polluted. However, the poisoning of the Thames had been a very gradual intermittent process, with its roots in the medieval period. Several centuries earlier, a network of rivers had run through London into the Thames from sources high in the surrounding hills. These rivers provided the obvious means to dispose of both sewage and industrial waste, which slowly turned them from pleasant waterways into filthy open drains. Keen to obscure these unsightly, foul-smelling watercourses from view, residents began to cover them over and thus London acquired its first underground tunnel network. Over the centuries, these rivers would be diverted deeper underground – still flowing silently beneath our feet to this day.

The London landscape looked very different before the rivers were closed off from view. Close to the River Lea, the forbiddingly named Black Ditch flowed through east London into the Thames at Limehouse. The sacred Walbrook ran through the centre of the Roman city of Londinium, where the occupying soldiers worshipped at the Temple of Mithras. The Fleet and the Tyburn rose at rural Hampstead and streamed past the villages that surrounded the northern and western edges of the metropolis. The River Westbourne provided a pleasant place for travellers to rest their livestock at Bayard's Watering Place (modern Bayswater) before flowing into Hyde Park, where Queen Caroline dammed its waters in 1730 to create the Serpentine. Further west, Counter's Creek and Stamford Brook provided water for the inhabitants of the ancient settlements we now know as Chelsea and Hammersmith.

South of the Thames, the Falcon meandered through the common land of Wandsworth and Clapham while the Effra's course led from Norwood, through the villages of Dulwich and Brixton, down to the Thames at Vauxhall. Today, the Imperial War Museum conceals the source of the River Neckinger, which flowed through south-east London (possibly joined by two tributaries – Earl's Sluice and the Peck) before forking into two rivulets that formed a watery boundary to the notorious rookery of Jacob's Island.

London's rivers had become dangerously contaminated by the Middle Ages. As early as 1290, the prior of a Carmelite monastery in Whitefriars complained of how members of the brethren had succumbed to miasmas rising from the Fleet. In addition, the Walbrook was constantly choked by refuse thrown into its waters by the numerous skinners practising their craft on its banks. The Common Council endeavoured to rectify the problem, making leaseholders of land surrounding the riverbanks responsible for keeping the waterways clear of filth.

Nevertheless, the Fleet and the Walbrook grew more choked and foul smelling with every year that passed. In order to obscure the revolting sight of the fetid waters flowing through their midst, landowners began to pave over parts of the rivers. In his *Survey of London* published in 1603, John Stow wrote of the Walbrook, 'This water course having diverse Bridges, was afterwards vaulted over with bricke and paved levell with the Streetes and Lanes where through it passed, and since then also houses have been builded thereon, so that the course of the Walbroke is now hidden under ground, and thereby hardly knowne.' It was the first of London's rivers to vanish from view.

The River Fleet remained above ground for some years more, although it was generally perceived as a blight on the city. By the 1600s it was referred to by Londoners as a 'ditch' rather than a river, its central section impassable due to use as a dump for butchers' refuse. Numerous clean-up attempts were made throughout the century, but each time the Fleet quickly refilled with rotting viscera and sewage. Its muddy banks became treacherous to pedestrians and rumours abounded of unwary individuals slipping into the slurry. One particularly grisly story related the fate of a barber from Bromley, Kent, who, after a drunken night out at a City hostelry, fell into the Fleet. He was found the next day standing upright in the mud, frozen to death.

By the early 1700s the authorities had admitted defeat and attempts to clean up the Fleet were abandoned. Respectable families living close to its banks fled to more salubrious climes and the once-pleasant riverside properties degenerated into slums. The area surrounding the Fleet Ditch at Clerkenwell became one of London's worst rookeries, packed with dilapidated lodging houses occupied by thieves and other undesirables. According to local legend, the worst of these lodging houses stood at the corner of Brewhouse Yard. Commonly referred to as 'Jonathan Wild's House', after the notorious thief-taker, it contained myriad hiding places and escape routes for villains on the run. Trapdoors were concealed in cupboards and behind curtains, through which felons could disappear into the murky depths of the Fleet. The ditch also provided a handy place to dispose of incriminating evidence, which quickly sank into the mud.

The Fleet became nothing more than an open sewer and the decision was made to henceforth conceal it from view. In 1735, the section running from Ludgate Hill to Holborn Bridge was covered over and a marketplace was laid out on the new land. A quarter of a century later, work began to cover the remaining part of the Fleet that lay within the city boundaries. By 1768, virtually the entire river – from Holborn to the Thames – had been forced underground.

Despite the problems caused by the dreadful state of the Fleet and the Walbrook, London's waste still had to be disposed of. The rivers' convenient habit of carrying deposits to the Thames, where they were dragged out to sea by the tide, meant that they remained the favoured method of refuse removal. All manner of rubbish found its way into the city's waterways, but the most revolting was undoubtedly human waste. Originally, Londoners had dealt with the disposal of sewage themselves, quietly spreading it on their gardens or surreptitiously dropping it into the nearest drain. However, by the 1300s, the sheer volume meant it was impossible to dispose of it personally. As a result, men were employed as 'rakers': freelance workers who removed the contents of household cesspits. The first recorded mention of a raker dates from 1327, while 30 years later a civic document declared, 'The dung that is found in the streets … shall be carried … out of the City … by the Rakyers.'

However, the onerous task of emptying the cesspits was often left to the householders. In 1535, London physician Thomas Vicary wrote, 'The Raker … shall have a horne, & blowe at every mannes doore … to lay owt theyre offal.' Some rakers were willing to do the job themselves for more pay, most notably the unfortunate 'Richard le Rakyere' who, in 1326, fell into a cesspit he was emptying and drowned.

Once the raker had filled his cart he would drive out to the countryside, where his unsavoury product was sold to farmers who found it to be excellent manure for their crops (particularly those of the root vegetable variety). In 1816, Solomon Baxter, owner of Potteral's Farm in North Mimms, Hertfordshire, took out advertisements in the newspapers extolling the benefits of human excrement for turnips, which apparently 'came up very luxuriantly, and continue uncommonly strong and healthy'.

Due to the nature of their business, London's rakers were increasingly obliged to carry out their work after dark to avoid complaints from neighbours. By the mid-1700s they became known as 'night soil men', with local bylaws passed to ensure their business was conducted in a discreet and sanitary manner. The night soil men were forbidden to offload the contents of their carts in built-up areas and had to adhere to strict rules as to when collections could be carried out. For example, in the parish of St Clement Danes, fines of up to £5 could be issued to any night soil men caught 'beginning to empty any bog-house, or taking away night soil, at any time, except between 12 at night and five in the morning'.

For centuries, the valuable (if nauseating) work of the rakers or night soil men ensured London's rivers remained relatively free of household sewage. However, by the 1700s the whole idea of domestic cesspits was being questioned. Traditionally, even the smartest houses had privies close to their backdoors for ease of use, particularly in the cold winter months. Some homes even had indoor facilities with cesspits dug underneath their ground floor. Almost without exception, these pits were not enclosed and so, consequently, the effluent leaked into the surrounding soil, producing an aroma that pervaded the house, particularly on hot summer days. As London's streets became more densely populated and the smells worsened, so it became clear that waste had to be taken away from the buildings. As a consequence, homes began to attach drains to their cesspits which led, via sewer pipes, to the nearest river.

By the end of the 1700s, rivers in previously rural areas had begun to fill with waste. It became clear that it was only a matter of time before they suffered the same fate as the Fleet and the Walbrook. By 1827, the section of the Westbourne that ran from Hyde Park to Sloane Square had become such a hazard that it was covered over and built upon. Less than 10 years later, it was considered too filthy to continue providing the water for Queen Caroline's Serpentine lake. In 1854, doctors petitioned the sewer commissioners to conceal the remaining part of the river that ran from Sloane Square to the Thames, after numerous local residents succumbed to a devastating cholera epidemic everyone suspected was linked to the stinking river. By this time, the Westbourne was generally referred to as the 'Ranelagh Sewer' – an apt description of the foul stream that ran through lands in Chelsea once owned by the wealthy Earl of Ranelegh.

Although many people would have preferred to see the rivers cleaned rather than driven underground, the sheer quantity of waste produced in the capital by the beginning of the 1800s made their fate inevitable. Even an attempt by Lord Kensington to turn the filthy Counter's Creek into a canal, in the 1820s, turned into a commercial disaster when the canal quickly silted up, making it impossible to navigate. Only 30 years after it opened, the canal was sold to the West London Railway, who diverted the creek underground and laid railway tracks in the old canal bed.

By the late 1820s, the population of London reached over 1.3 million as the Industrial Revolution drove thousands of ex-agricultural workers into the city in search of work with the new manufactories. As the city expanded, the dangers associated with dumping industrial waste in the rivers became manifest. On 25 January 1828, *The Times* warned, 'Accounts are constantly appearing in the newspapers … establishing beyond doubt the great impurity of the Thames water taken up at London. The Commissioners of Sewers have endeavoured to prevent the refuse of the gas works from escaping into the river, but from the immense quantity now used, it inevitably finds its way thither. I am assured that the refuse water discharged into the Fleet ditch sewer at Battle Bridge, which runs into the Thames, is equal to that of a gutter on a rainy day; forming a perpetual stream of poisoned fluid, and depositing a green sediment upon the stones over which it passes. Not long ago it was proved upon trial, that a horse was actually poisoned by drinking water impregnated with the refuse of the gas-works in the Horseferry Road.'

Horses were not alone in succumbing to poison. The newspapers were inundated with reports from concerned passers-by who had seen huge quantities of dead fish floating in the Thames. Londoners realised it was not only the sewers and manufactories that were polluting the river. For many years, the huge enclosed docks that ran along the banks of the Thames had been discharging all manner of chemical and industrial waste into their vast basins, where it was inevitably dragged into the river as the tide receded. On 28 August 1828, newspapers carried the tragic story of William Nurse of Charles Street, Westminster, who died after falling into the West India Dock's export basin. Witnesses to the accident were certain the poor boy had been poisoned by the huge amount of copperas (iron sulphate) released into the water by the copper-bottomed boats that berthed there.

In addition to spewing toxic chemicals into the Thames, the sewers themselves could be highly dangerous places. Three months after the death of William Nurse, the residents of College Street, Cowley Street and Wood Street in Westminster were thrown into panic by loud explosions emanating from a sewer leading from the gasworks in Great Peter Street. Eyewitnesses watched in horror as huge flames leapt from the drain grating, almost knocking a man off his feet as he walked out of the nearby Bull's Head pub.

On a lighter note, concealment of the rivers underground shrouded them in mystery, with tall stories and incredible sightings abounding. In 1836, *The Gentleman's Magazine* related one such story that had been doing the rounds for 100 years: 'A fatter boar was hardly ever seen than one taken up this day coming out of the Fleet Ditch into the Thames. It proved to be a butcher's, near Smithfield Bars, who had missed him five months, all of which time he had been in the common sewer, and was improved in price from 10 shillings to two guineas.'

During the 1700s, the positioning of London's sewers had been dictated by geography. The ancient rivers provided the main channels leading to the Thames, to which manmade drains were connected. However, as nature's sewage system struggled to cope with the sheer amount of waste relentlessly piled into it, the authorities tried to introduce order to the labyrinth of stinking waterways now flowing beneath their feet. By 1834, seven trusts had been set up in the capital with responsibility for maintaining the underground sewers. Six of the trusts controlled areas north of the Thames, namely Westminster, Holborn and Finsbury, Blackwall and Poplar, the City of London, Tower Hamlets and Regent Street. Only one single trust was responsible for sewers in south London, managing a massive area stretching from the River Ravensbourne in Kent to the Ember branch of the River Mole in Surrey.

By this time, the majority of West End and City households had drains connected to the river sewers. This made them major contributors to the increasingly dreadful state of the Thames, but the fact that their sewage was carried away meant they were generally in a much finer state of health than their neighbours in east London.

In poverty-stricken districts such as Bethnal Green and Shoreditch, the way the inhabitants disposed of their waste had not changed for centuries. As late as the 1840s, Bethnal Green had 33 miles of streets (not including the innumerable courts and alleys) and just seven and three quarter miles of sewers. Here the night soil men, long since made redundant in the West End, found plenty to employ them. The impoverished residents invariably disposed of human waste in the same manner as the Elizabethans, throwing it into gutters or spreading it over the few gardens that existed in this densely populated neighbourhood. Occasionally, the council would build a sewer along one of the main thoroughfares but it would remain virtually unused, as few householders could afford to have their home connected to it. Consequently, disease was rife, particularly in the old slums tucked away behind the major roads, where access to drainage was impossible. In these places waste was left to fester, contaminating local water supplies and attracting disease-carrying vermin.

Dr Hector Gavin, a Fellow of the Royal College of Surgeons, studied conditions in the East End in the mid-1800s and began to suspect the local population were being poisoned by their water supply. On a trip to the Hackney Road (an area where disease was rife), he examined several communal water tanks and was horrified at their contents, later writing, 'one contained the remains of fish, in a putrescent state; the wood of the second was rotten, covered with green, slimy mould, and the surface of the water iridescent from the scum floating on it; the third was an open kind of horse trough, adjacent to the privy.'

In addition to contaminated water tanks, Gavin also found many East End residents were living in conditions not seen in wealthier areas for decades. Many homes still had open drains running directly under the ground floor, and some cesspits were so full that their contents oozed over the boards of the outhouse, forcing any visitor to stand in raw sewage. In a couple of locations, filth had spread out of the privy and the unfortunate tenants resorted to dumping ashes in its path, in a vain attempt to stop it creeping into their home.

Given this deplorable state of affairs, it might have been assumed that landlords of sewage-ridden properties would feel obliged to employ the services of night soil men. However, this was not the case. As Hector Gavin explained, 'when it is considered that the usual cost of cleansing cesspools in London is £1 each time, and that the rents of the dwellings of the poor range from one shilling to … five shillings a week, it can be readily understood that the poor cannot cleanse their cesspools and privies, and that the landlords consider the expense very oppressive, and consequently neglect the operation.'

Of course, if the landlords had cared about the living conditions of their tenants and connected their homes with the main sewers, the situation on the River Thames would have been even worse. As it was, the river was in such a filthy state that, by 1855, the London waterworks was banned from supplying its customers with water taken from the tidal reaches of the Thames. However, a few forward-thinking politicians and civil servants saw the situation as an opportunity rather than a nuisance. One such man was Charles Pearson, solicitor to the City of London.

By the time of the Great Stink, Pearson had been working for the City in various capacities for over 40 years – including a stint chairing the Board of Health from 1831-33. During his time in office, he had been horrified by the living conditions that prevailed in less affluent areas and had resolved to improve the lives of the City's poor. He also had firsthand experience of the summertime miasmas emanating from the Thames, as his home was just a few minutes' walk from the riverbank in Park Street, Westminster. As the state of the river reached crisis point in June 1858, Pearson urged his peers to force Parliament into action. But ridding the city of the river-borne stench formed only a small part of his master-plan. Pearson's subsequent campaigning on behalf of London's poor would, in less than a decade, transform the terrain that lay beneath the streets for ever.

While Charles Pearson formulated his grand plans for the City of London, his contemporaries searched in desperation for a way to clean up the Thames. Eventually, a possible solution emerged from across the English Channel. For decades, Paris had periodically been enveloped by unbearable stenches emanating from the Seine. However, in 1850, Baron Haussmann oversaw the construction of new sewer and water supply networks under the city, reputedly rendering the once filthy river clean enough to wash fine linen in. As London continued to suffer under the riverside stench, *The Times* cried in despair, 'If the English engineers are not up to it, let's send for a Frenchman.'

CHAPTER 2

THE UNDERGROUND VISIONARY

As fate would have it, *The Times*' plea for a Frenchman was not ignored. During the Great Stink, the man in charge of the capital's public engineering works was one Joseph Bazalgette, grandson of Jean Louis Bazalgette – a wealthy tailor from Ispagnac, France who had arrived in England in 1784.

Joseph was born in 1819 in Enfield, Middlesex to Joseph William Bazalgette, an officer in the Royal Navy, and his wife Theresa. At the time, Enfield was a sleepy market town beyond which lay acres of fields and woodland, providing a perfect playground for Joseph and his sister. However, shortly before his 10th birthday, the family moved away from the open, airy countryside into the urban heart of London. At first they took a house at 5 Lower Lisson Street, just off the Edgware Road, but soon moved to 48 Hamilton Terrace in the exclusive enclave of St John's Wood.

Now living in the grimy and overcrowded metropolis, Joseph was exposed to the appalling living conditions endured by London's poor. Just a short walk away from his home, behind the bustling thoroughfare of Edgware Road, were the labyrinthine street slums of Lisson Grove. This forgotten part of London had been ignored when the smart houses of Marylebone were fitted with new, sweet-smelling drainage systems, still languishing amid the stench of cesspits in the backyard until well into the middle of the 19th century.

Such sights were to have a profound effect on Joseph Bazalgette's professional life. Unlike contemporaries such as Charles Dickens and Henry Mayhew, however, he did not choose to help the poor by exposing their desperate living conditions through the written word. Instead, he was to give more practical assistance by using his engineering skills.

By the time he was in his early twenties, Bazalgette had qualified as a civil engineer and set up offices at Great George Street, Westminster, close to the home of City solicitor Charles Pearson. At the time, Britain was in the grip of railway mania and Bazalgette soon became inundated with work drawing up plans for new tracks, stretching the length and breadth of the country. His practice prospered and by 1845 he had acquired sufficient personal wealth to propose to Maria, the daughter of a rich Irishman named Edward Keogh. One year later, their first son was born and his new family gave Bazalgette further incentive to make his fledgling engineering business succeed. With little mind to his own wellbeing, he took on project after project until, in 1847, the massive workload overwhelmed him and he was forced to leave London for a long recuperative break.

This bout of mental exhaustion suggested the relentless work and financial precariousness of self-employment did not suit Bazalgette's constitution. Indeed, a contemporary description of him as 'very slight and spare, and considerably under the average height' does not suggest a man destined for greatness. However, Bazalgette's return to London in 1849 started a chain of events that would ultimately make him one of the founders of London's underground labyrinth.

In the August of that year, Bazalgette was appointed assistant surveyor to the Metropolitan Commission of Sewers. This government body had long been wrestling with the problem of how best to dispose of London's sewage, but had failed to find a solution. Consequently, in the year prior to Bazalgette's engagement, the Commission was receiving an average of 100 complaints a week from disgruntled ratepayers. In October 1849, *The Times* came to the sorry conclusion that, 'This sanitary council is wholly inefficient and useless.' After staggering on for another six years and achieving very little, the Commission was scrapped, while a new body (the Metropolitan Board of Works) was created in its place. Joseph Bazalgette was retained as its chief engineer.

At first, the new board seemed to be following in the weary footsteps of its predecessor. For two years following its inception, very little was achieved apart from relentless repairs to old sewer pipes and countless meetings to discuss the best way forward, prompting the public to christen the new council the 'Metropolitan Board of Words'. However, the stench of the Thames during the summer of 1858 forced the government to pour funds into the board's coffers and finally, with sufficient money at his disposal, Bazalgette sprang into action.

The problem faced by Joseph Bazalgette and his team was truly massive. By the middle of the 19th century, London stretched for miles and comprised thousands of homes and businesses, the waste of which ultimately ended up in the Thames. The most popular solution was to resurrect the old practices of the night soil men and use the sewage as agricultural manure. Enthusiastic members of the public submitted plans to the Board of Works, showing how a series of gigantic pipes running to the suburbs could divert waste away from the Thames toward the market towns of Hertfordshire, Essex and Surrey. However, the draughtsmen of these grand schemes failed to take into account that London was situated in a valley and, as such, gravity would simply not permit their ideas to work.

Bazalgette knew that recycling the city's sewage was impractical, expensive and virtually impossible to engineer. So, instead of getting rid of the problem, he decided to relocate it. Anyone watching the progress of flotsam and jetsam on the central part of the river could see it was little affected by the tide. Junk floating on the surface sometimes remained visible for days, only moving a few feet as the tide flowed in and out. However, further downriver, towards the Essex border, tides were stronger and refuse deposited near the riverbank at Barking disappeared with the first high tide it encountered. Realising that sewage deposited at this point in the river would quickly vanish, Bazalgette began to draw up his plans.

The second problem was how to stop underground rivers and drains from disgorging their contents into the central London stretch of the Thames. To change their course would have been hugely expensive and disruptive, so instead Bazalgette resurrected an idea for the contents of the old sewer system to be diverted before reaching the river. After studying the routes of the existing system and the volume of sewage that passed through it, he decided that a total of five intercepting sewers should be built, each running west to east across London.

Three of the new sewers were planned north of the river, rather unimaginatively christened the High Level, Middle Level and Low Level Sewers. The High Level Sewer would begin at Hampstead and run seven miles along the perimeter of the metropolis, draining Highgate, Kentish Town, Holloway, Hornsey, Stamford Hill, Stoke Newington, Homerton and Hackney. Further south, the Middle Level Sewer would start at Kensal Green and run under the Regent's Canal at Paddington to Notting Hill, where it would continue its subterranean journey east through Bayswater and down Oxford Street. After coursing its way under this major thoroughfare, the sewer would travel through Holborn to Clerkenwell Green and thence to East London via Old Street and Shoreditch. From there, it would follow the line of Bethnal Green Road and Green Street towards Bow, where it would join the High Level Sewer.

The disruption caused by laying the Middle Level Sewer through the crowded districts of Oxford Street, Clerkenwell and Bethnal Green presented problems for Bazalgette, but its low-level neighbour posed an even greater challenge. Its western branch was planned to drain the comparatively quiet areas of Acton and Hammersmith, from whence it would travel towards Pimlico, under Lupus and Bessborough Streets, until it reached the northern foot of Vauxhall Bridge. From this point Bazalgette and his team concluded that the sewer had to travel in a line parallel to the Thames, in order to drain the densely populated West End. Therein lay a huge problem, however. One option was to lay the sewer under the Strand and Fleet Street, but these roads were so busy that any major long-term building works would be prohibitively disruptive. The alternative was to run it along the bank of the Thames, but this option too posed a very different set of problems. At the time, the riverbank from Westminster to Blackfriars Bridge looked completely different to today's urban vista. The river rose and fell across expansive mudflats that stretched towards the elaborate gardens and terraces of some of London's most sought-after properties.

The land on which these houses were built had once been London's most prestigious residential district. From the 1400s onwards, palatial properties occupied by high-ranking clergy and wealthy landowners lined the Strand. The back gardens of these palaces commanded unrivalled views across the Thames, with many featuring water gates from which the residents could climb aboard elaborately decorated private barges to take them up and down the busy river on excursions, whether for private pleasure or commercial reasons.

By the time Bazalgette and his team began to survey the area, the Strand had ceased to be fashionable, although some prestigious properties remained. At the western end lay a broad-fronted Jacobean mansion called Northumberland House. This property was the ancestral London home of the Percy family, one of England's wealthiest aristocratic dynasties, and as such was designed to make an impression on all who visited. Set around a stone courtyard, the square building was divided up into several apartments used by various members of the family and their servants. At the back of the building lay fabulously opulent staterooms, including a beautiful drawing room panelled with glass, designed in the 1770s by celebrated architect Robert Adam. The glass walls reflected the light that flooded in from the formal gardens, which stretched away from the property and afforded superb views of the river.

Robert Adam had also been involved in the construction of another development affected by Bazalgette's scheme. Nearly 100 years before the

Board of Works began to survey the area, Adam and his brothers built what was arguably their finest work – the Adelphi Terrace, overlooking the Thames slightly west of Waterloo Bridge. The Adelphi was constructed on the derelict site of Durham House, an ancient palace boasting an impressive lineage of owners including Elizabeth I and Sir Walter Raleigh. In its place, the Adam brothers built an elegant terrace of 24 brick-fronted town houses embellished with classical stucco ornaments. The first floors of these graceful four-storey homes featured balconies overlooking the river. Inside, the rooms were decorated with classic Adam fireplaces, surrounded by intricate ceiling and wall-plaster embellishments.

The main rooms of the Adelphi Terrace houses stood high above the riverbank. Beneath them lay 'cottages' for staff, beyond which arched stables led out onto a riverside landing stage where barges could unload their cargoes.

The Adelphi landing stages were not the only access points to the watery mudflats along this part of the Thames. In the mid-1800s, the riverbank was littered with small jetties and ancient quays, interspersed with stairs leading to the water's edge. Salisbury Stairs were situated close to the site of today's Cleopatra's Needle; York Buildings Stairs lay at the end of Buckingham Street; the modern Hungerford Bridge begins at the site of the old Hungerford Stairs; and Whitehall Stairs lay at the end of what is now Horseguards Avenue.

Sandwiched in between these steps to the river was Montagu House, the imposing London residence of the fantastically wealthy Duke of Buccleuch. His family had owned property on the site since the early 1730s and, by the time Bazalgette arrived on the scene, the Fifth Duke, Walter Francis Montagu Douglas Scott, had just finished building a new mansion in the style of a French château, with a stunning garden terrace leading down to the river.

As Bazalgette drew up his plans for the route of the northern Low Level Sewer, he realised that some land would have to be sacrificed by owners of the Strand properties (including the owners of Montagu House). The question was, how much of it?

While the Board of Works deliberated over the best route for the Low Level Sewer through Westminster, Bazalgette continued drawing up plans further east. It was decided that the three northern intercepting sewers would meet at Abbey Mills, near Stratford, where the sewage would be pumped into huge 9ft outfall pipes that carried the waste to Beckton, where it would be stored in a massive reservoir until it was disgorged into the Thames at high tide.

With the northern plans settled, Bazalgette turned his attention to south London. This side of the Thames was, fortunately, not as populous and only two intercepting sewers were required. The High Level Sewer would comprise two branches emanating from Clapham and Dulwich and drain a 20 square mile area taking in Tooting, Streatham, Clapham, Brixton, Dulwich, Camberwell, Peckham, Norwood, Sydenham and part of Greenwich. Its low-level counterpart would run through Wandsworth and Battersea to the Brixton Road, then on to Deptford where it would join the High Level Sewer. The combined contents would then be pumped up to an outfall sewer, in turn taking the waste underneath Woolwich town centre and across the Erith Marshes to Crossness, where it would be emptied into the Thames via a reservoir mirroring that on the north side of the river.

Today, it is difficult to imagine the sheer complexity and scale of Joseph Bazalgette's grand sewer project. Although relatively simple in principle, the actual works were a logistical nightmare that involved the purchase of acres of land from numerous private owners, the overseeing of a workforce numbering thousands, the purchase of materials from hundreds of suppliers, and the delivery and storage of those materials. Coupled with these challenges was the inevitable disruption of the communities through which the great sewers would run.

Considering Bazalgette had suffered a breakdown from overwork during the railway boom, he was either brave or foolhardy (or possibly a combination of both) to take on a project of such magnitude. But if there was any trepidation on his part, he kept his fears to himself.

In the first months of 1859, the Metropolitan Board of Works received the green light from Parliament after securing funding of £3,000,000 from the Bank of England. The first part of the monumental scheme was construction of the northern High Level Sewer. Contractors experienced in tunnelling were invited to tender for the project, which included the purchase of all building materials and the hiring of workers. Following careful consideration of tenders and the provision of sureties to ensure companies would remain solvent for the duration of the works, Bazalgette and his board awarded the project to William Moxon, a 40-year-old building contractor from Dover who calculated he could complete the work at a cost of £152,430.

The task taken on by Moxon was both challenging and labour intensive. With very little effective tunnelling equipment available, the sewers had to be built using the 'cut and cover' method, which involved excavating huge cuttings of about 30ft deep and shoring them up with timbers placed along the sides and across the top to stop earth falling in. Once the trench had been secured, the sewers (which could reach a height of 11ft in places) were built by laying bricks in either a circular or egg-shaped formation, starting with the bottom half and then covering over the top before refilling the sides of the trench with earth. Every time the new pipe met one of the old sewers it was intercepting, a junction had to be carefully created so that the contents flowed smoothly away without leaking and contaminating the surrounding earth.

Construction was carried out largely by hand, although steam engines were hired to aid with heavy lifting and gunpowder was employed to loosen the rock through which any tunnel had to pass. Consequently, Moxon had to employ hundreds of men to complete the project.

Many of the labourers who worked on the sewer construction sites were navigators, commonly known as 'navvies', who had gained much experience of this type of work through building Britain's network of canals. The navvies were a hardy bunch of itinerant workers who travelled on foot to wherever a large civil engineering project was going on. They drank as hard as they worked and had a fearsome reputation. Back in the 1830s, the engineer Peter Lecount described the navvies he came across as 'banditti', claiming, 'they are as complete a class by themselves as the Gipsies. Possessed of all the daring recklessness of the Smuggler, without any of his redeeming qualities, their ferocious behaviour can only be equalled by the brutality of their language. It may be truly said, their hand is against every man, and before they have been long located, every man's hand is against them.'

The navvies' tough reputation meant they often led quite isolated lives, having little to do with the communities in whose midst they temporarily worked. Consequently, they were a tight-knit group who, despite their fondness for drink, organised themselves extremely efficiently. All navvies were self-employed men who enjoyed the freedom it gave them. Fathers brought their sons into the trade as young as nine years old, so that they could learn the ropes by helping onsite, greasing the wheels of the barrows and taking tools to be sharpened at the local blacksmith's forge. The navvy community also looked after its own: if a navvy turned up at a site where no work was available, his colleagues would often give him a shilling apiece to sustain him until he found employment.

In rural districts, navvies often lived in temporary shacks erected by the contractor close to the site. In urban areas, such as central London, they would find the cheapest lodgings they could. Due to their peripatetic lifestyle, the men carried few possessions with them. For most, a pick and shovel, a 'tommy bag' for food and a tin teacup were all that was required, as food, drink and replacement clothing were usually provided by the contractor.

On arrival at a new job, the navvies either worked independently or organised themselves into groups who negotiated a fee for taking on a specific job. These groups were known as 'butty gangs' and were favoured by sewer contractors such as William Moxon, as the cost of the work could be fixed. (The modern Oxford English Dictionary definition of 'butty' is 'a confederate, companion or mate'. Probably a slang term, its usage was first recorded in the early 19th century.) The butty gangs were extremely proud of their skills and regularly boasted they could excavate huge sections of trench and tunnel without need of an engineer. They each had a leader (or foreman) who was responsible for making sure his men arrived for work on time and completed the job as quickly as possible, in return for a larger slice of the fee. Some of the more adventurous English butty gangs travelled to the USA during the American railway boom, where their name was corrupted into 'buddy' – still used today to describe a friend or companion.

Once sufficient butty gangs and other labourers had been taken on at a site, excavation of the cutting could begin. Much of the work was done by hand, with hundreds of men shovelling earth into barrows pulled away from the works by horses. Navvies referred to the materials they excavated as 'muck', regardless of whether it was soil, rock, clay or chalk. As the cutting got deeper, the navvies were lowered into the trench in skips operated by banksmen, who were also responsible for lifting the heavy muck out of it. These skips were operated by a pulley system powered either by steam engines or horses, and the banksmen had the responsibility of ensuring they were lowered and extracted safely. It was essential that the ropes were regularly checked, as if one snapped under the weight the skip would fall into the cutting, injuring or possibly killing the men trapped inside.

In addition to the skips, muck was removed from the cuttings by barrow – probably the most arduous task faced by the navvies. First, the muck-face was worked on by 'getters', who drove their picks into the impacted earth until it was loose enough to be shovelled into the barrows. Sometimes the layout of the works meant the barrows sat above the height of the area being cleared, while navvies had to lift their laden shovels above their heads to deposit the muck. Once this exhausting part of the excavation was complete, the barrows were pushed by 'muckshifters' up steep planks to the top of the cutting. For particularly heavy loads, a rope was attached to the barrow and tied to a horse at the top of the trench to help the muckshifter get it up the slope.

If navvies needed to tunnel through rock, they formed a crew with the most experienced man, known as the 'tunnel tiger', at the helm. The tiger worked out where gunpowder should be placed in the rock-face and supervised while the holes were drilled by a 'spannerman' (who held the drill up) and a 'hammerman' (who pounded the drill with a huge mallet). Once the holes were drilled, the tiger filled them with charge and cleared the area in preparation for the blast. The resulting shower of rock was then transported from the cutting in barrows and skips.

Navvies continued this exhausting, repetitive work for up to 12 hours a day, six days a week. Saturday afternoon was looked forward to with great enthusiasm, as not only was it the end of their week but also when the navvies got paid. The complicated process of remunerating hundreds of men was taken on by an employee of the contractor, each of whom had their own system. In 1867, journalist James Greenwood witnessed a navvies' payday which he later described in his book, *Unsentimental Journeys*:

'Every man is provided with a tin ticket, which bears a number corresponding with one put against his name in the time and pay books. On Saturday, the navvy gives in this ticket enclosed in a little canvas bag, highly branded with the number. In the course of the day, and undisturbed in his little office, the pay clerk makes up the account, and his assistant pops the proper sum into each bag and secures it with its string. Come pay time, the navvy army troops past the pay hole, and as the clerk calls out the number, the bag is deposited on the ledge and is taken up by the owner. The tin ticket also serves another purpose. If his work is satisfactory, the navvy finds the ticket in the bag along with his money; if however, his services are no longer required, the ticket is retained, and the navvy trudges off for good and all.'

Supervision of navvies, clerks and their assistants fell to the contractor's agent, a highly trusted member of staff in charge of seeing the entire project through to its completion. In return for this huge responsibility, which included adherence to the budget agreed for the work, the agent was paid a fee plus a share of the profit. If he was able to complete a task under budget he was often permitted to keep the residual money, or sometimes given a bonus incentive to finish the work quickly.

Unsurprisingly, a position as a contractor's agent was much sought after. Although it carried a certain amount of responsibility, the buck ultimately stopped with the contractor himself – whose position was not for the fainthearted or disorganised. Although the potential existed to make a massive amount of money, contractors had to be expert at selecting trustworthy and knowledgeable agents, and also had to be, above all, good at delegating work. Many contractors of public works during the Victorian period simultaneously took on numerous projects across the vast British Empire and beyond, employing thousands of workers from countries whose language and culture were not understood, forcing them to place total trust in their agents. The agents' business was stressful and precarious, their reputation only as good as their last project.

One of the most prolific and successful contractors of the period was Thomas Brassey, a self-made man from Cheshire who won the contract to construct the northern Middle Level Sewer shortly after work on its high-level counterpart commenced. Brassey's working methods were nothing short of astounding, considering that for much of his career he employed an average of 80,000 people across four continents. With this size workforce, it would be reasonable to assume he spent his working day in a sizeable office complex, surrounded by managers, clerks and secretaries. In fact, he had no office staff, nor even an office, preferring to commit the details of each project to memory and to write all correspondence himself.

In theory, Brassey's eccentric working practices seemed like a short route to career suicide. By 1847, however, he had personally overseen the construction of nearly a third of all British railways – a fact that never ceased to amaze and confound his competitors.

As Thomas Brassey prepared for work on the northern Middle Level Sewer, contracts were issued for numerous other facets of Bazalgette's grand project. Responsibility for the construction of the southern Low Level Sewer was given to the firm of John Aird & Son of Lee in Kent, while the task of completing the northern Low Level Sewer (with the exception of the west London branch and the problematic central section) was awarded to another resident of Lee, William Webster.

Webster later won the contracts for the southern reservoir and the southern outfall sewer after Rowland Brotherhood, who had come in with the lowest tender, had to pull out after being unable to secure sureties. In the excitement of winning such a prestigious contract, Brotherhood had recklessly ordered a massive consignment of bricks from the Smeed brickworks in Sittingbourne. When his sureties were not forthcoming, he desperately tried to cancel his order but by this time Smeed had already made half of it. Some 14,000,000 bricks subsequently had to be sold at a loss and a furious Mr Smeed sued the beleaguered Mr Brotherhood for the deficit.

Luckily, no other brick makers suffered the same problem as the unfortunate Smeed. In fact, one made a small fortune from Bazalgette's sewers: George Furness, owner of the Willesden Brick & Tile Company, was also a civil engineering contractor who worked on a wide variety of projects, ranging from the British railways to the rebuilding of Odessa after the Crimean War. He was awarded the complex task of building the northern outfall sewer, which involved constructing two huge pipes 9ft in diameter and carrying them above ground through east London, over streams, railways and streets via aqueducts. Obviously Furness had no problems in obtaining the bricks, eventually making a significant profit from the long and complicated job. He ploughed much of it back into his business and his bricks can still be seen today in much of Willesden's late 19th-century housing stock, on streets such as Odessa Road and Furness Road (named in deference to their maker).

While the Metropolitan Board of Works were busy selecting contractors from the numerous tenders they received for each part of the project, building work on the first part of the scheme, the northern High Level Sewer, carried on apace. By the beginning of 1860, this colossal pipeline had reached Stratford – the meeting point of the entire northern sewer network.

Across the river, building works also began on the high-level pipeline but, despite the contractors' best efforts, things did not go as smoothly as hoped. From the project's inception the press had published the cost of each stage of work, and the figures quoted gave Londoners severe cause for concern. The projected cost of the southern outfall sewer alone was set at a massive £300,000, as residents began to worry that their domestic rate bills would rocket in order to pay for it. Discrepancies in the quantity surveyors' reports also gave cause for concern, as people began to suspect that in some cases more building materials were being ordered than necessary.

The cuttings that were now appearing on both sides of the river also bothered the public. In July 1860, local residents began to lose patience with the Board of Works when a huge trench along Florence Terrace, on New Cross Road, lay idle for five weeks while traffic and pedestrians struggled to negotiate it. One month later, Deptford town centre ground to a halt when several roads were closed so that the path of the southern High Level Sewer could be excavated. The work was originally started by a subcontracting firm named Hellings & Yeoman but, after a few weeks, it became clear that the work was running woefully behind schedule. While Bazalgette's team at the Board of Works feverishly searched for a contractor who could speed up the project, the gaping holes in Deptford's roads lay open for eight weeks, maddening shopkeepers who experienced a serious downturn in trade. Mr Wheatly, the local omnibus proprietor, complained he was losing £50 per week through having to reroute his vehicles.

For the remainder of the year, the sewer works continued to exasperate anyone who lived or worked near them. Roads became impassable, mud oozed across the streets and householders were forced to put up with constant noise during daylight hours. There was little respite even at night, as hard-drinking navvies crowded into local pubs for evenings of rowdy entertainment that often ended in violence. In September 1860, William Smith and John Carter, who had both been working on the northern High Level Sewer, got into a drunken argument over a woman at a pub in Bow. A ferocious fight ensued, during which Smith was kicked so hard that he had to be taken to hospital.

While navvies worried the locals with such boisterous antics, they also inadvertently made one poor man's life a misery. On 7 December 1860, a harassed surveyor named William Moxon wrote in desperation to *The Times* from his office in Trafalgar Square: 'The similarity of our name, the circumstance of our business pursuits sometimes running in the same channel, and the fact that ever since the high-level sewer was commenced I have been inundated with navvies out of work, and have received threatening notices from the owners of adjacent houses, all prompt me to explain that I am not in any way connected with Mr William Moxon (the sewer contractor).'

At this point in the proceedings, faced with an unruly workforce, angry residents, delayed works and spiralling costs, Joseph Bazalgette must have wished that he had never started the sewer project. However, although 1860 was fraught with problems, he did finally decide how to drain the congested areas of the Strand and Fleet Street. But in doing so, he was to incur the wrath of one of Britain's most wealthy and influential men.

By July 1860, it became clear that, following extensive surveys of the area, the only sensible route for the northern Low Level Sewer would be via the proposed embankment stretching from Queenhithe to Westminster. Not only was this route a good deal less disruptive than digging up the Strand, it would also provide a surface on which a new road could be built, thus providing a much-needed alternative route into the City. In order to fund this innovative but expensive scheme, Bazalgette suggested that the wine and coal import duties, which were due to expire the following year, were renewed. This would bring in estimated revenue of around £100,000 per annum, which could be used to offset the projected £1,000,000 it would cost to build the embankment. This proposal was submitted to Parliament and Bazalgette sat back and anxiously waited for their response.

In the meantime the New Year brought with it more problems, some of a far more serious nature than fighting navvies or disgruntled shopkeepers. In February 1861, the dangers of working in the sewers became all too apparent when four navvies – John Devaney, Daniel Horigan, Patrick Ryan and Alfred Ward – were found lying dead in the Fleet sewer. The four men had been sent into the ancient tunnel to make repairs for connection of the intercepting sewer. However, unbeknown to them, as they worked a nearby factory began to pour chemical waste down its drains. It ran down the pipes, emitting a deadly gas as it did so. The first indication the navvies had of its presence was a choking stench of rotten eggs, but by then it was too late to escape. Trapped in the claustrophobic, stinking tunnel, they were overcome by the lethal fumes of hydrogen sulphide. The awful nature of their deaths shocked press and public alike but, amazingly, the factory owner was not rebuked and continued to dispose of toxic waste by throwing it down the drains.

Repairs to the existing sewers also caused problems of their own. On 6 June 1861, 'J.T.' of Anchor Street in Bethnal Green complained to *The Times* that his house had flooded with sewage following the installation of an inadequately sized sewer pipe connecting his property with the new main drain. He lamented, 'Ankle deep in filthy water, the servants were obliged to wade to remove carpets and furniture … when the water subsided, the odour may be imagined.'

Throughout the 1860s, many Londoners still believed that diseases such as typhoid and cholera were carried via foul-smelling air and so the vents leading to the new intercepting sewers became a cause of great concern. People living or working near them feared they would be exposed to deadly diseases. The outcry became so great that the Board of Works set up a commission to experiment with ways to deodorise the vents. Various techniques were tried until it was agreed that the most effective solution was to place charcoal filters inside the openings, which effectively dispelled the unpleasant aroma.

Although the sewers were avoided by the majority of London's population, some of its more daring inhabitants were lured into the murky tunnels by greed. In July 1861, George Wicks and Daniel McKeogh were caught heaving large, grease-covered sacks out of the sewer in Southwark. When the police investigated their contents, it was found that they were filled with tallow – animal fat used in the manufacture of candles and soap. The tallow had escaped into the sewer during a fire at a nearby factory, but had subsequently been bought by a Mr Harradine for the bargain price of just four shillings per hundredweight, in return for him clearing out the sewer. On learning this, Wicks and McKeogh protested, they had gone to work on behalf of the tallow's original rightful owner. Their hastily prepared story was not believed by the court and they were each sentenced to one month's hard labour.

Two months after Wicks and McKeogh had been caught stealing the tallow, the smartly dressed ladies of Victoria Street were terrorised by 'two ragged urchins' named Shipwright and Davis, who spent a jolly afternoon rolling clay from the nearby sewer cutting into balls and hurling the muddy projectiles at local shoppers. The two lads were duly arrested and taken to the House of Correction for seven days, as punishment for their tomfoolery.

Although the first few months of 1861 were fraught with bad publicity, much work on the sewers was completed over the summer months. By the beginning of October the project was in full swing again, with around 6,000 navvies working on the various levels of pipework both north and south of the Thames. In north London, William Moxon had almost completed the High Level Sewer. Thomas Brassey's men were working on three sections of the Middle Level Sewer at Old Ford, Bayswater and Oxford Street. George Furness was halfway through construction of the complicated overground outfall sewer, building foundations for the aqueducts and lowering the North Woolwich Railway between West Ham and Plaistow so that the pipes could be carried above it.

Over in south London, the two branches of the High Level Sewer running from Clapham and Dulwich to New Cross had been completed. William Webster's men were making excellent progress on the southern outfall sewer, which took the form of an enormous conduit 12ft in diameter, running from Deptford through Woolwich and over the Erith Marshes to the proposed reservoir at Crossness. This immense pipeline was finally completed at the end of April 1862 and, in order to celebrate, Webster invited 500 local dignitaries and members of the Board of Works to a banquet. However, this feast was not to be held in a West End hotel or the local town hall – it was to take place in the sewer itself.

On the afternoon of Monday 5 May 1862, the slightly apprehensive guests assembled outside St Alphage's Church in Greenwich, where they were led to a narrow access chamber via a long ladder. One by one they descended into a surreal subterranean world. The immense circular pipeline had been given a temporary floor so that it resembled an extremely long, arched crypt. The floor extended for a mile along the tunnel and was lit on either side by lamps, flickering against the red brickwork. In the centre of the floor a huge, narrow table laden with food stretched into the gloom, an unforgettable sight made all the more extraordinary by how this unique and oddly beautiful banqueting hall would soon be obscured from view forever.

Just two weeks after William Webster's eccentric banquet, Joseph Bazalgette threw a party of his own, inviting various London luminaries and gentlemen of the press to survey the work being done on the northern outfall sewer. *The Times* described the site in great detail: '500,000 yards of concrete, 20,000 rods of brickwork, 800,000 bushels of cement and 100 million bricks will eventually be used in the construction … Tramways are laid along the whole line of the work for conveying the materials … five locomotive engines are constantly in use, and 500 trucks, while employment is given to about 2,300 men, forming the contractor's staff. Dotted here and there along the line are mills for making concrete, one of them turning out as much as 360 yards of concrete a day … [We] made a minute inspection of the whole works … walking for that purpose through miles of sewers with lighted candles [and] conveyed in ballast trucks to and fro along the remainder of the line, Mr Bazalgette explaining by the way all the various points of interest.'

Both Bazalgette's and Webster's tours gave some much-needed positive publicity to the controversial sewer works. However, just four days after the visit to the northern outfall sewer, disaster struck. On 28 May 1862, tons of earth from the cutting at Church Street, Shoreditch fell through the pavement, fracturing a gas pipe beneath. The escaping gas then came into contact with a steam engine being used by the navvies, causing it to blow up. The massive explosion caused carnage. Mr Hayes' boot and shoe shop at 151 Church Street collapsed, trapping passer-by Jane Smith inside the smouldering debris of the building, where the unfortunate woman's clothing caught alight and severely burned her. All the buildings from 146 to 154 Church Street had their glass and doors blown out, with Mr Mannings, a haberdasher at number 150, narrowly escaping the same fate as Jane Smith.

Although Bazalgette and his colleagues were no doubt hugely disconcerted by the dreadful accident at Shoreditch, they soon had a much stickier problem to overcome: namely William Henry Walter Montagu Douglas Scott, the Sixth Duke of Buccleuch. As MP for Midlothian, the Sixth Duke was fully aware of Bazalgette's proposed embankment of the Thames at Westminster. He also knew that the roadway along its top would run right through the back garden of Montagu House, his London residence, blocking his direct access to the Thames.

The Duke had a great fondness for his London house, not least because it provided an easy walk to his work at the Palace of Westminster. Desperate to retain his riverside garden, he first tried to block plans for the Embankment altogether and then, when the project seemed certain to proceed, offered to pay £90,000 a year to keep the river frontage from Whitehall Palace to Westminster private.

This offer outraged London's general public. For decades the Strand and Fleet Street had suffered from terrible traffic congestion, and people could not believe the Duke was trying to scupper a remedy to the problem for the sake of a small part of a huge garden he used for only a few weeks a year. 'It would be an infinite pity if interests so unimportant as are [the Duke of Buccleuch's] were to be allowed to stand in the way of an interest so great as that of the public,' a correspondent calling himself 'Scotus' wrote to *The Times*. 'This great man has six magnificent houses and lives but a short time in any one of them. For the sake of some little gratification of taste to him and his family for a month or two of the year, to have the vast body of the people deprived of a convenience great and constant, is surely not to be endured. One's blood boils to think of such a thing.' Thankfully, Parliament agreed with Scotus and Bazalgette's plan for the Embankment, including the controversial roadway, was approved.

The new embankment, which was to be named after the reigning monarch Queen Victoria, would extend up to 400ft into the previously unusable, boggy riverbank and would be lined with granite. Running at an average of 4ft above the waters of the Thames, its surface would comprise a 70ft roadway and two 15ft pavements beyond which would lie pleasant public gardens providing a much-needed respite from the choked atmosphere of the Strand. Beyond this, the private properties that lined the riverbank (including the Duke of Buccleuch's mansion) would each receive at least 100ft of additional land at the end of their gardens, although of course they would lose direct access to the river.

Hidden inside the embankment would be two huge tunnels measuring approximately 9ft in diameter – one carrying the Low Level Sewer, the other for utilities. There would also be room for additional tunnels, which got Bazalgette's old neighbour, Charles Pearson, thinking.

In the meantime, the Board of Works set about selecting contractors for the construction of the Victoria Embankment. The job was eventually split between George Furness, William Webster and a new contractor, Anthony Ritson, who took on the construction of the section from Waterloo Bridge to Temple Gardens.

By the beginning of 1863, every facet of the grand sewer project was underway. The two High Level Sewers were finished, Brassey & Co had begun work on the northern Middle Level Sewer and the complex sections of the northern Low Level Sewer were edging towards completion. Aird & Son had begun the southern Low Level Sewer, while Webster continued to press on with the southern outfall works and the reservoir at Crossness. By the summer, Furness had finished the northern outfall reservoir and, on 20 July, a party was held to celebrate the first time that sewage from the High Level Sewer was emptied into the Thames at Barking.

This reservoir, like its slightly smaller counterpart across the river, was a masterpiece of engineering. It covered 10 acres and was 17ft deep, capable of holding 39 million gallons of sewage. Buried underground, its surface was covered by a wide plateau of soil dotted with ventilation shafts fitted with the Board of Works' deodorising charcoal filters. Underneath, the basin of the reservoir was divided into four sections, each fitted with two sets of sluice gates – one to admit the sewage from the outfall pipes, the other to let it out into the Thames at high tide.

In July 1864, a journalist was invited by Furness to go and view one of the unused sections, later writing, 'It really presented a wonderful sight. In height and in the general position of its brick columns and the spring of its arches it was not unlike the crypt of the Guildhall, but the daylight was excluded, and its vast area was only indicated by little rows of coloured lamps, which marked the outlines of the columns and curve of the arches, and which, twinkling away in the long, dark, silent distance till they became minute points of fire and nothing more, gave the whole dim interior an aspect which was at once novel and solemn in the highest degree.'

By March 1865, every part of Joseph Bazalgette's monumental sewer network was complete, with the exception of the Victoria Embankment. On 4 April, the scheme was formally opened when the Prince of Wales started the engines of the pumping station at Crossness to lift the contents of the southern outfall sewer into the vast reservoir. This auspicious occasion was attended by the cream of British society, including eminent scientists and engineers, politicians, high-ranking civil servants, archbishops and several members of the aristocracy, such as the Duke of Cambridge and Prince Alfred.

On the morning of the official opening, the royal party travelled from Charing Cross to Crossness in two special trains. On arrival, they were first taken across the river by boat to view the northern reservoir. Although the exhibit had been kept free of sewage, the smell was so dreadful that guests retreated to the boat with handkerchiefs pressed firmly to their noses.

The Prince of Wales and his retinue then travelled back across the river to Crossness Pumping Station, where an assembled crowd of dignitaries had been waiting for them. A group of navvies had gathered on the bank of the reservoir to watch proceedings and they gave His Royal Highness loud cheers as he disembarked from the boat and made his way to start the great pumping engines. In truth, their cheers should have been reserved for Joseph Bazalgette, whose engineering genius, combined with a genuine concern for his fellow Londoners, had improved – and in some cases prolonged – the lives of countless inhabitants of the city.

With the rest of the sewer network now complete, the only piece of the project that remained unfinished was perhaps the most impressive – the Thames Embankment. The Embankment was taking a long time to build for a variety of reasons, particularly the completion of pipes for the utility tunnel that lay above the sewer. This useful tunnel would house numerous pipes belonging to London's waterworks and carry numerous subterranean conduits for the fuel that had revolutionised the way in which streets, homes and businesses were illuminated – gas.

London had led the world in the adoption of gas lighting. As with the groundbreaking sewers, however, it had been the brainchild of a man of continental European descent. Not long after Bazalgette's grandfather, Jean Louis, emigrated to England, Friedrich Albrecht Winzer arrived in London from Brunswick, Germany. Although neither a scientist nor an engineer himself, Winzer was a talented entrepreneur. During the first years of the 19th century, he noted with great interest how several of the huge cotton mills in the north of England had installed lighting powered by coal gas. By keeping the looms illuminated long after the sun went down, the gaslights had massively increased the mills' output. Thus far, however, the method had not been adopted by many southern businesses.

Winzer realised that gas lighting could be rolled out on a grand scale, providing illumination not just for businesses but also for streets and private houses. Reasoning that London, the marketplace of the Industrial Revolution, would be the perfect place to launch such a service, he cannily changed his name to the more English-sounding 'Frederick Winsor', applied for patents for gas-making equipment and purchased a site in Mayfair, on which he intended to build London's first gasworks. Winsor then set about raising funds to realise his plans by selling shares in his newly established National Light & Heat Company. Advertisements were placed in the press extolling the virtues of coal gas: 'This gas flows cold and transparent as air, in any tubes, to any place, and burns clearer and brighter than wax or oil. It may light all rooms, halls, shops, streets, squares, roads and coasts, and serve as fire and light for every culinary purpose.' Should potential investors have still been unsure about purchasing shares in the company, Winsor gave demonstrations of the gas in action at his office at 97 Pall Mall, every Monday, Wednesday and Friday at 8pm.

Although his approach to fundraising was both creative and energetic, Winsor's weakness lay in exaggerating the potential return on investment. The enthusiastic entrepreneur claimed in his advertisements that backers could expect an annual return of £6,000 for every £50 subscribed, while the projected profits would be so vast that they would contribute to relieving the national debt. These ridiculous projections did little for Winsor's credibility and, unsurprisingly, he failed to raise sufficient capital to get his idea off the ground. However, his talent for promotion did bring the concept of gas lighting to the attention of the City. In 1810, a group of investors led by businessman James Grant established the Gas Light & Coke Company; within only five years, London would contain 30 miles of gas mains and similar projects were planned across Britain.

Despite the instant popularity of coal gas, it failed to bring Frederick Winsor the riches he dreamed of. Although he was originally taken on as a director of the Gas Light & Coke Company, his unrealistic attitude to finance, combined with an excitable personality, ensured he was quickly ousted. Dejected but undeterred, Winsor travelled to France and attempted to set up a similar company in Paris. It quickly failed and he finally lost interest in gas as a fuel.

Frederick Winsor never returned to England, dying in Paris in May 1830. However, his onetime colleagues in England had not forgotten the eccentric German gentleman who first brought gas light to their attention through his peculiar experiments in Pall Mall. Shortly after his death, subscribers erected a memorial to him in Kensal Green Cemetery. The monument, topped by a sculpture of a flaming torch, bore a fitting inscription from the prophet Zechariah: 'At evening time it shall be light.'

CHAPTER 3

CHARLES PEARSON
AND THE SUBTERRANEAN RAILWAY

Although almost all of Joseph Bazalgette's subterranean sewer network was up and running by 1865, the final piece of the project – the Thames Embankment – remained under construction for another five years. This was not because of problems with the sewer, or even the utility tunnel, but due to the integration of a scheme that was to revolutionise the way that Londoners travelled around the city: the underground railway.

'The Tube', as it later became known, was the brainchild of Bazalgette's old colleague, Charles Pearson. In his capacity as solicitor to the City of London, Pearson was all too aware of the overcrowded, insanitary conditions endured by many residents of the districts surrounding Westminster and the City. Many of these areas' inhabitants were forced to live in squalid, damp, draughty houses shared by several families, some in rooms no larger than 10ft square. The writer John Hollingshead described some of these districts in his book *Ragged London* (1861):

'In the west there is Knightsbridge, rendered filthy and immoral by the presence of its large military barracks ... in the south there are Lambeth, Walworth, embracing Lock's Fields, and the Borough, with its notorious Kent Street; in the north there is Agar Town, built on a swamp, and running down to the canal in every stage of dirt and decay, with Somers Town, Kentish Town and Camden Town, each contributing its share to the general mass of misery; and in the east there are St Georges, Whitechapel, Bethnal Green and overgrown Shoreditch.'

Many properties in these districts had no access to piped water or sanitation. Dank basements overflowed with sewage following heavy rainfall; broken windows were patched with rags; refuse rotted in the gutters. Consequently, many residents living in the midst of such filth suffered from chronic ill health. In 1849, Henry Mayhew interviewed a woman from Bermondsey about her living conditions. Her response revealed the root of the problem: 'Neither I nor my children know what health is ... but what can one do? We must live where our bread is.'

In fact, very few inhabitants of London's overcrowded surrounding districts wanted to stay there. They had no option, however, as they had to live within walking distance of their place of work. But as the railways made their inroads into London in the late 1830s, Charles Pearson began to develop a revolutionary idea that would finally free the working poor from their unsanitary surroundings. By 1846, he had developed his concept into a workable scheme which he presented at the City's Common Council chambers in the Guildhall on 11 May.

Pearson's proposal involved the creation of a suburban village for 'persons of the middle and lower classes' on the rural outskirts of the city, to be connected with their places of employment by an underground railway. This new line would enter London near King's Cross, cross the New Road leading to Paddington and run parallel with the Gray's Inn Road before veering east towards Farringdon Street, where Pearson envisaged the construction of a new 'Grand Central Railway Terminus'. Much of the railway would be built on land already earmarked for slum clearance. In its place, Pearson would build a 'spacious and handsome street, 80 feet in width', lined with terraced houses. The track would run at basement level along the centre of the thoroughfare, arched and paved over with openings in the roadway and footpath to provide light and ventilation.

Pearson's novel proposition attracted sufficient interest for it to be put before a House of Lords committee considering proposals for London railway termini. Frustratingly, however, the committee rejected the scheme, fearing that the construction of an underground railway would be prohibitively expensive. In addition, many people did not share Pearson's enthusiasm for the suburbs, thinking them devoid of character and inferior to the city in every way. This opinion was espoused by John Murray in 1841, when he wrote a scathing piece for *Blackwood's Magazine*:

'The suburbs ... have a character peculiarly their own; once seen, they cannot be mistaken. They are marvellously attached to gardening, and rejoice above all things in a tree in a tub. They delight in a uniformity of ugliness, staring you out of countenance with five windows in front, and a little green hall door at one side, giving to each house the appearance of having had a paralytic stroke; they stand upon their dignity at a distance from the road, and are carefully defended from intrusion by a bodyguard of spikes bristling on a low wall. The natives of these places are less wealthy than genteel ... they are eloquent on the merits of an atmosphere charged with dust, which they earnestly recommend for inhalation, under the attractive title of "fresh air". All shopkeepers, tradesmen and others in these regions are insufferable bad and dear.'

Although his concept of a railway to connect workers with a suburban idyll had been rubbished, Pearson remained convinced it was the only conceivable way of solving the chronic problem of overcrowding in the city. Undeterred, he pressed on with his campaign and was soon heartened to hear of problems being faced at the terminus of the Great Western Railway at Paddington.

Unlike termini closer to the City, such as London Bridge, the location of the Great Western's London station caused great problems for its passengers. Despite the presence of the New Road (now the Marylebone/Euston Roads) connecting it to King's Cross, the journey from Paddington into the City was slow at best and downright excruciating at busy periods. In response, a Bayswater, Paddington & Holborn Bridge Railway scheme was devised, which proposed running an underground line from Paddington station down the New Road to King's Cross, before continuing to Holborn via Pearson's proposed route.

This new railway would effectively link Paddington with the City, and could also take passengers arriving at Euston and King's Cross stations. The proposal caught the attention of City investors, who knew only too well how congested the New Road became at peak hours, and the North Metropolitan Railway Company was formed to actively promote the scheme. Very soon after its formation, the company would drop 'North' from its title, creating the name by which London's first Tube line is still known today.

Thus Charles Pearson's idea was hijacked by the Metropolitan Railway. In a bid to attract more investment, his Grand Central Terminus at Farringdon was axed on the grounds of expense and potential disruption. Instead, the company concentrated on wooing influential backers, in particular Rowland Hill – the great reformer of the postal system – who was persuaded that the new railway could expedite distribution of the city's mail.

At this point, it would have been understandable if Pearson had walked away from the project a bitter man. However, his genuine concern for the working class deterred him from self-pity. He continued to tirelessly campaign on behalf of the railway, asserting that its creation would have a profound effect on the demographic structure of London. In a pamphlet dated 1859, he stated:

'The decennial census, and the reports of the officers of health and of the visiting clergy in the city, record the fact that our courts and alleys are crowded with a stagnant mass of human beings of the lowest class intermingled with the families of respectable working men, who have the means to migrate, like their masters, if they had facilities which a railroad would afford them, and to live with their families in the country, a few miles from the locality of their occupation.'

Pearson's campaign worked. By 1860, sufficient funds had been raised for building of the Metropolitan Railway to commence. Sir John Fowler, a no-nonsense Yorkshireman with much experience of railway projects, was appointed chief engineer with two contractors working under him – John Jay, who was responsible for the line east of Euston Square, and Smith & Knight, who took on construction work for the western section. Fowler designed the railway to run almost entirely underground from Paddington to Euston beneath the route of the New Road. This entailed digging up the thoroughfare, which would cause a huge amount of congestion. Once the line reached the more built-up areas that lay east of Euston Square, Fowler proposed laying the tracks in a deep cutting through some of the most deprived areas of the city, conveniently sweeping away some of London's worst slums.

The construction process for the pioneering underground railway was very similar to that of the sewers being built at the same time. Frederick Smeeton Williams described the arrival of the contractor's men at King's Cross in his book *Our Iron Roads* (1860):

'The work of constructing this remarkable railway eventually became, as it must be allowed, somewhat wearisome to the inhabitants of the New Road. A few houses on wheels first made their appearance, and planted themselves by the gutter; then came some wagons loaded with timber, accompanied by sundry gravel-coloured men with picks and shovels. A day or two afterwards a few hundred yards of roadway were enclosed, the ordinary traffic being, of course, driven into side streets; then followed troops of navvies ... who soon disappeared within the enclosure and down the shafts. The exact operations could be but dimly seen or heard from the street by the curious observer who gazed between the tall boards that shut him out; but paterfamilias, from his house hard by, could look down on an infinite chaos of timber, shaft holes, ascending and descending chains and iron buckets which brought rubbish from below to be carted away; or perhaps one morning he found workmen had been kindly shoring up his family abode with huge timbers to make it safer. A wet week comes and the gravel in his front garden turns to clay; the trades people tread it backwards and forwards to and from the street door; he can hardly get out to business or home to supper without slipping, and he strongly objects to a temporary way of wet planks, erected for his use and the use of passers-by, over a yawning cavern underneath the pavement.'

The first few months of work on the new subterranean railway were marred by disaster. On 31 May 1860, a Great Northern train carrying passengers from Liverpool, Manchester, Sheffield and Huddersfield failed to stop when it reached the buffers at King's Cross. *The Times* reported: 'dashing at full pace through the station, [it] actually leaped the platform ... a height of five or six feet, carrying with it the tender (the carriage containing the water and fuel for the engine), the break, and one or two carriages, and, proceeding on its fearful and precipitous course, ran down the inclined plane immediately under the clock tower and across the Old St Pancras Road, burst through the enclosure of the Metropolitan Railway works, and, but for the immense quantity of earth lying there, would have buried itself in the shaft of that undertaking.'

Incredibly, no one was badly injured in this spectacular accident. The fireman, one Mr Church, managed to jump out of the tender with seconds to spare, and although the driver, Thomas Annis, stayed with his engine until it crashed, he walked away from the scene with barely a scratch. It was the unfortunate passengers who bore the brunt of collision with the earthworks (although again, none were badly hurt): Mr Randall, who had been travelling back to his home at Little Knightrider Street, cut his knee open; George Earnshaw of Huddersfield and Charles Cooper of 9 Catherine Street, Lambeth both suffered lacerations to their heads; Mrs Edwards of Lambeth Road was 'conveyed to her residence very much contused'.

Unhappily, fate was not on the side of victims of a further accident outside King's Cross station, six months later. George Wiggins, an engine driver, and Charles Tann, a stoker, were both killed instantly when the engine on which they worked suddenly blew up. Despite attempts to establish the cause, nothing could be found to confirm the engine was faulty. Wiggins and Tann's colleagues said the men were paying full attention to their work and had not reported any problems before the explosion. It remained a mystery and, to his great relief, contractor John Jay was not held responsible.

Despite these two accidents, building of the Metropolitan Railway continued uninterrupted. By September 1861, work was underway on virtually every section. The line from Paddington station to an ancient tavern at Bayswater (known as The Yorkshire Stingo) was finished. The section running underneath the New Road to Euston was being completed with little disruption, although it was feared that two of the elegant houses in Park Crescent might have to be demolished to accommodate it.

The road leading from Great Portland Street to Euston was swarming with navvies hard at work on the deep cutting. Between King's Cross and

Farringdon, it had been necessary to issue compulsory purchase orders on numerous houses, many of which the locals were pleased to see demolished due to their dilapidated state. However, hundreds of residents in the streets that branched off the Gray's Inn Road were made homeless by the works. As the railway was not yet finished, these unfortunate tenants were unable to act on Charles Pearson's suggestion and seek new homes in the suburbs. Instead, they were forced into the roads that surrounded their previous abodes, which then became even more crowded than they were before.

The eastern section of the Metropolitan Railway proved the most complicated part of construction. In addition to cutting a swathe through the Fleet valley by demolishing numerous buildings, John Jay's men had to tunnel through a hill of clay at Clerkenwell and pick their way through centuries of subterranean pipes in this densely populated part of town. As Smeeton Williams noted in *Our Iron Roads*: 'the bed of a London thoroughfare has been compared to the human body – full of veins and arteries which it is death to cut. No sooner is the ground opened than these channels of gas and water, of sewers and telegraphs are seen as close together as the pipes of a church organ. The engineers of the Metropolitan Railway had, to begin with, to remove these old channels to the sides of the roadway, and then to cut their way between with the delicacy of a surgical operation.'

Sometimes these detailed works were fraught with problems, but none were as soul-destroying for the workers as the incident at Clerkenwell in June 1862. Heavy rain in the area between Ray Street and Saffron Hill caused water in the Fleet sewer to swell until it burst out of its confines into the adjacent railway works, its massive torrent causing bricklayers working in the cutting to flee for their lives. As the trench filled with stinking water, men armed with pickaxes were lowered down in baskets in an attempt to knock holes in the newly built brickwork, thus allowing water to escape into the surrounding earth. However, after just a few minutes it had to be abandoned, as the foundations began to collapse. The last man had barely reached the top of the cutting as several hundred yards of arched tunnelling came crashing down into the seething waters.

While the contractor's team cleared the Clerkenwell site and prepared to painstakingly rebuild the collapsed tunnel, works along the other stretches of line and the stations carried on apace. In August 1862, Fowler and his two contractors invited investors and members of the press to inspect how they were progressing. At three o'clock on the afternoon of Monday 5, the party assembled at the partially complete station squeezed into the back of the

Great Western Terminus at Paddington, facing Bishops Road (now Bishops Bridge Road) and adjacent to the Grand Junction Canal. After being shown around the site, they were introduced to arguably the most important element of the Metropolitan Railway – its first engine. The fact that much of the new railway was underground made the traditional steam-powered engines totally unsuitable for use, as their smoke and steam would have quickly enveloped tunnels and stations in a thick, choking fog. Consequently, Fowler and his team would design a new engine capable of retaining smoke and vapour while the train was in a tunnel, and releasing them when it reached an open cutting.

Attached to the engine were what closely resembled standard railway carriages, except that their interiors were more spacious and had a higher roof than normal. The shell was constructed from wood to create a long, thin compartment accessed by several narrow, half-glazed doors. Inside, the carriages were furnished with seating which was skilfully (if riskily) illuminated by ingenious gas lights. An anonymous *Times* journalist who attended the inspection visit described how the gas lighting worked:

'The mode in which the gas is conveyed is very simple and most efficacious. Along the roof of the carriage is a timber trough some three feet wide by two high. In this is enclosed an India-rubber bag, capable of containing gas enough to feed the two lamps placed in every compartment for two or three hours. A weighted board is laid inside the case over the bag, in order to keep the feed of gas at an equal pressure from first to last. When empty, the bag, or reservoir, is replenished in a few minutes from an ordinary gas stand pipe.'

Although this method of lighting an underground railway carriage would have modern Health & Safety executives up in arms, at the time it had been tried and tested on several overground railway lines without incident. The only concern raised by the journalist was how the lights generated a lot of heat in the carriage, thus making summer travel stiflingly hot.

Once aboard the carriages, the invited guests set off on the inaugural journey at an average speed of around 12mph. As the train slowed on approach to the first station at Edgware Road, passengers became aware of the rumble of street traffic above them – an indication that the 'cut and cover' method of construction did not take the tunnels far underground. The station itself was (and still is) above ground, affording a welcome break from the claustrophobic darkness of the tunnel. Its most notable features were a handsome roof constructed from glass and iron, to protect waiting passengers from the elements, and plenty of seating.

From Edgware Road, the party departed to the first of the stations built entirely underground – Baker Street. Here, the train emerged from the blackness of the tunnel into a broad station illuminated by shafts of light beaming down through arched openings in the roof, evoking a vaguely churchlike atmosphere. (Something of the original feel of this groundbreaking station would be restored in the 1980s, when the site was subject to major renovation works. Today, passengers standing on the Circle Line platforms can catch a glimpse of how London Underground's first stations would have looked.)

The guests attending the tour in August 1862 were unable to journey further than King's Cross, as the Fleet valley section of the line had been held up due to the destruction caused by the escaping waters of the Fleet sewer. However, by the following January the entire line from Paddington to Farringdon was ready to open to the public. To mark this auspicious occasion, the platform of Farringdon station played host to an 'elegant *déjeuner*' to which over 600 people were invited. The guests all arrived at the station after a tour of the line, taking their seats along three rows of elegantly dressed tables stretching down the platform. Above their heads, hundreds of flags and banners fluttered under the curved roof, which was festooned with white and scarlet swags. The top table, reserved for the most eminent guests, stood at one end of the platform on a raised dais. Here sat Mr W. A. Wilkinson, chairman of the Metropolitan Railway, alongside Lord Mayor Rowland Hill, several aldermen and Members of Parliament. However, one notable figure was absent: Charles Pearson.

Tragically, Pearson, the underground railway's most energetic champion, had succumbed to the effects of dropsy six months earlier. He died without reward for his lengthy, tireless campaign to inaugurate London's subterranean railway. After refusing the Metropolitan Railway Company's offer of financial recompense for his efforts, Pearson did not even receive the satisfaction of seeing his brainchild realised. However, the company did not forget what this great man had done for them and, shortly after his death, granted his widow Mary an annuity of £250 a year.

More important than financial recompense was that the Metropolitan Railway did exactly what Pearson wanted it to: running a quick and affordable form of transportation for ordinary Londoners. During rush-hour periods the trains ran at 10-minute intervals, reducing to every 20 minutes between the hours of 11am and 4pm. The railway was also cheap, with passengers travelling in first-, second- or third-class carriages and even first-class tickets costing less than omnibus fares over the same distance. Most importantly, the railway ran special trains for working people that started from both ends of the line at 6am and 6pm. Passengers using these trains could travel the entire length of the line for just one penny, prompting *The Times* to note, 'These trains will be a real boon to poor people, labourers and others, who have now often to walk many miles to their work.'

The wheels had been set in motion for the great exodus of the working class from inner-London slums, as the Metropolitan Railway proved an instant success. From the moment it opened to the public, queues formed outside the ticket offices. By 8am the line was running at full capacity and, by the end of the day, it was estimated that around 25,000 Londoners had used the groundbreaking service.

However, underground travel was not an altogether pleasurable experience. Back in the 1840s, *Punch* magazine had poked fun at the railways by describing a typical journey. It is fair to assume that little had changed by the time the Metropolitan Railway opened, and even modern commuters will be able to relate *to Punch*'s wry warning about third-class carriages: 'Do not expect the luxury of a seat. As an individual and a traveller, you are one of the lower classes; a poor, beggarly, contemptible person, and your comfort and convenience are not attended to.'

Punch's criticism was not confined to third-class travel, however, as it advised patrons of all three classes: 'You pay nothing extra for civility, so you must not hope for it. Remember that you are at the mercy of the Company as to where you may stop for refreshments; for which, accordingly, be not surprised if you have to pay through the nose.'

In addition to a distinct lack of comfort, Fowler's engines were not quite as effective at retaining smoke and steam as had initially been hoped. On the day the line opened, two harassed travellers protested: 'it was understood that there was to be no smoke or steam from the engines ... All we can say is, that on one of the journeys between Portland Road and Baker Street, not only were the passengers enveloped in steam, but it is extremely doubtful if they were not subjected to the unpleasantness of smoke also.'

The gas lighting in the carriages also posed a problem. The lamps worked very well while the train was stationary but, when it began to move, their flame flickered so much that reading a book or newspaper was practically impossible. In addition to its poorly lit, smoky atmosphere, the underground railway inexplicably lacked station signs. Passengers unfamiliar with the line had to call out to guards on the platforms, or rely on the knowledge of their fellow passengers, to establish which station they were at.

Despite these problems, the underground railway (and its affordable tickets) was hugely and immediately successful, prompting other countries to consider the possibility of subterranean travel. Even before the London railway had opened, Emperor Napoleon III had engaged Fowler and his team to build a similar line between Montmartre and the Louvre, which would form the first part of the Paris Métro.

Back in London, the success of the Metropolitan Railway prompted calls to connect all the capital's mainline termini with a subterranean line. As a result, in early 1863 Sir John Fowler drew up plans for what would eventually become the Circle Line. The engineers' proposed route would use part of the existing line from Paddington to Farringdon. From these points, however, the new line would turn southwards, passing through the City in the east and Kensington in the west before turning back towards Westminster, to form a complete circuit around the periphery of central London.

The sheer size and complexity of the new underground project made it potentially too much for the Metropolitan Railway to finance and oversee on its own. Consequently, a new company was formed, known as the Metropolitan District Railway, which took on construction of the line from South Kensington to Tower Hill, a challenging and complicated section of the route destined to cause widespread problems – not least for Joseph Bazalgette, who was still trying to complete his sewer project.

Despite the anticipated problems of building the line, demand for more underground railways was such that both the Inner Circle line (as the new line was called) and the first stretch of what would become the District Line, connecting the Inner Circle with the above-ground West London Railway at West Brompton and Addison Road (now Olympia), were approved by Parliament.

With the finance quickly raised, the Metropolitan District Railway began work on the Kensington section of the line in 1865. The work was as complex and problematic as predicted. Many cuttings had to be over 40ft deep to ensure wealthy residents were not disturbed by the passing trains and a tunnel had to be blasted through Campden Hill, provoking a huge amount of disruption. However, the residents of Leinster Gardens in Bayswater paid probably the greatest price for the coming of the underground railway. This well-to-do street was lined with tall terraces of elegant, stucco-fronted houses, just a short cab drive away from the West End and Knightsbridge. Little did local families know that, at the beginning of the 1860s, their peace would be shattered when Fowler and his team chose their quiet street as the location for a large cutting, where subterranean engines could expel their smoke and steam.

Numbers 23 and 24 Leinster Gardens were earmarked for compulsory purchase to create the tunnel opening and, for a while, it looked like the impressive terrace would need a hole knocked through it to accommodate the railway. However, Fowler realised that this would ruin the look of the street and decided to retain the façades of the two houses, demolishing only the remaining parts of the properties. To this day, the fronts of these houses obscure the deep cutting that lies behind their front doors.

By the time the Inner Circle had made its way through Kensington, the Metropolitan District Railway had begun to run out of money. Their railroad's route through Westminster utilised Joseph Bazalgette's Victoria Embankment and, as funds dwindled, they pleaded with the Board of Works to cease construction on the final part of the sewer project until they had enough funds to continue with the railway.

By this time, Bazalgette's project had been underway for several years and the great engineer was keen to see it reach completion. However, work on the Embankment stalled as the two factions struggled to reach an acceptable compromise. Eventually, an irritated Bazalgette decided to press on with his work regardless. When sufficient funds had eventually been raised, the railway company were forced to re-excavate the Embankment wall in order to build their rail tunnel, which held up completion of the project even more.

The Victoria Embankment (as the Board of Works had now christened it) finally opened in May 1870, after a gargantuan effort on the part of the Metropolitan District Railway involving the labour of 2,000 men (including 300 on a night shift), 250 horses, 300 trucks, 130 barges and 20 steam cranes. The completed tunnel was 25ft wide and almost 16ft high, running for just under two miles with stations at Hungerford (Embankment), Norfolk Street (Temple) and Blackfriars. A grand opening ceremony was organised – although this became as fraught with difficulty as the building of the Embankment itself.

The Board of Works were delighted when Queen Victoria herself agreed to officially open their groundbreaking structure. Ten thousand tickets for this prestigious event were printed and contractors were commissioned to erect huge swathes of tiered seating along the roadway, leading up to a specially built royal pavilion in which the monarch would sit. Elegant young ladies, carrying colourful bouquets of flowers, would line the sides of the pavilion, while the unattractive pillars of the nearby Charing Cross railway bridge were concealed by a bank of evergreen trees. In preparation for the royal tour, the three underground railway stations were bedecked with flowers and flags while the railway company and the Board of Works waited in eager anticipation.

In the event, the Queen, who had been suffering a debilitating bout of depression, decided not to attend the event, sending instead the Prince of Wales and his daughter Louise, the Princess Royal. This disappointed the guests so much that, by the time the royal entourage arrived, some of stands were half-empty. The disappointment was made worse by the fact that the Metropolitan Board of Works had not given much thought to the transport they would use to accompany the royal guests on their tour of the two-mile structure. As *The Times* reported: 'the state portion of the procession was itself not particularly imposing, but the shabbiness and the ill-assorted carriages of the members of the Board of Works introduced an element of the grotesque which rendered the whole almost ridiculous'.

Although the opening ceremony of the Victoria Embankment seemed inauspicious, it did in fact mark a turning point in the life of the capital. Joseph Bazalgette had finally solved the centuries-old problem of how to dispose of London's sewage, potentially increasing the cleanliness of the city and the health of its citizens. Coupled with this was the underground railway which, although in its infancy, was poised to revolutionise the way people travelled around the metropolis. The subterranean city was expanding and, as its tunnels began their tentacular reach into the outer districts, so the population would follow them. Charles Pearson's vision was becoming a reality.

CHAPTER 4

THE SUBTERRANEAN CITY EXPANDS

The construction of the Metropolitan Railway and the intercepting sewers opened up a new world below Londoners' feet. Subterranean building projects had once been considered dangerous and prohibitively expensive, but men such as Joseph Bazalgette had proven this was not necessarily the case. Consequently, by the mid-1860s, the world beneath London had started to be put to all manner of uses – one of the first such being the Crystal Palace subway.

The Crystal Palace itself was an extraordinary structure resembling a huge, wonderfully elaborate greenhouse, originally used to house the Great Exhibition at Hyde Park in 1851. Once the exhibition finished, the venue was deemed too beautiful to destroy and so it was moved, piece by piece, to the top of Sydenham Hill, where it formed the elaborate centrepiece of a sprawling public winter garden opened by Queen Victoria in 1854.

The Great Exhibition had been a phenomenal success, and so the promoters of the Crystal Palace Winter Gardens expected their venture to draw a lot of visitors. In keen anticipation, a railway station serving the attraction was built on the slopes of the hill, connected to the Palace by an elegant glass colonnade. However, as soon as it opened one problem became obvious. Inside the colonnade lay a steep flight of over 100 steps, which visitors had to climb to gain access to the site. This laborious ascent had clearly not troubled the station's architects, but many members of the public found it discouraging to the extent that they did not return to the gardens. The precipitous steps also caused another problem: due to the massive amount of people using them, in wet weather they became absolutely filthy. Ladies attending the smart fêtes and concerts held on the grounds complained that their dresses were ruined before they even arrived at the venue, as their skirts had dragged across the mud-strewn steps.

By the early 1860s, it was clear that there needed to be another way of getting to the Palace by rail. A new station was designed at the top of the hill, with covered access to the Palace via a subway running from the station and under Crystal Palace Parade, before emerging at the entrance to the palace's ground-floor halls. The subway was designed to compete with the glass colonnade in aesthetic terms, and it did not disappoint. Reminiscent of a medieval monastery, its vaulted ceiling was supported by sturdy octagonal pillars faced in brick that opened out into a red and cream Byzantine design at the top.

The subway was cool, tranquil and accessible, and therefore generally expected to be a consummate success. However, by the time it opened, in 1865, the Winter Gardens were already losing their appeal. The station subway became virtually deserted on weekdays, as visitor numbers fell dramatically – although the great glass Palace struggled on until 1936, when it was destroyed by fire.

Thus was the usefulness of the Crystal Palace subway short-lived. However, at the same time as tunnelling works commenced at Sydenham, plans were underway for another tunnel that would prove far more successful.

During the early 1860s, London's docks were thriving, conveying cargo from the four corners of the globe to an increasingly consumerist nation. Most of the docks lay on the north side of the river and so were easily connected via the overground railways. However, numerous wharves were over on the south side of the Thames, along with the one of the port's largest enclosed docks – the Surrey Commercial. This sprawling network of deep basins stretched across the Rotherhithe peninsula and specialised in handling timber and foodstuffs, both of which were to be distributed nationwide.

The railway companies realised that a freight service running under the Thames, connecting the Surrey Commercial Docks and the south bank wharves with north London, would be both popular and lucrative. They began to investigate ways to achieve a new subterranean railway line, quickly realising that the answer already lay beneath them.

Over 30 years before Joseph Bazalgette began his sewer project, the great engineers Marc and Isambard Brunel had embarked on a doomed scheme to create an underground tunnel linking north and south London. The Brunels proposed a subaqueous passageway running from Wapping on the north bank of the Thames to Rotherhithe on the south. This ambitious subway would be large enough to accommodate horse-drawn wagons, which would gain access to the subterranean shaft via gently sloping ramps.

However, the scheme proved a disaster from start to finish. In order to excavate under the river, the Brunels designed a huge iron shield that was pushed up against the earthworks at the tunnel entrance. At the front of the shield were a series of timber boards stacked horizontally and held in place by screw jacks. The inside of the shield was divided into a framework of compartments large enough for a man to work in. Navvies climbed into each of these sections, removed one of the boards in front of them and began to dig into the soil. When a couple of inches of earth had been dug out, the board was put back into position. Once all of the boards had been moved, the frame of the shield was jacked forward. Bricklayers then entered the freshly dug section of tunnel and encased it in a thick brick lining.

Unsurprisingly, excavating a tunnel by means of nothing more than manual labour, a metal frame and a series of boards proved unbearably arduous, slow and dangerous. As the tunnel got deeper, the air quality got so bad that the navvies regularly passed out through lack of oxygen. In addition, the stinking slurry on the bed of the Thames (which had yet to be cleaned up by Bazalgette) regularly oozed through the tunnel walls, causing deadly build-ups of methane that caught light from the naked flames used by the struggling workmen. However, the biggest danger in the tunnel was the water that flowed above it. During the first two years of excavations, workers were forced to hurriedly evacuate the tunnel several times when water broke through the roof. Luckily, the speed at which it entered the site gave them time to escape, but, in January 1828, some of their colleagues were not so lucky.

On Saturday 12 January, Isambard Brunel arrived at the works early in the morning, just as the day shift was taking over from the night gang. He made his way into the tunnel, which now stretched well under the Thames, and climbed up into the top compartment of the shield where two men, named Ball and Collins, were working. As soon as he got near the shield face, Brunel noticed that the earth seemed much looser than normal. However, before he had time to consider whether it posed a danger to his workmen, the river broke through the tunnel roof.

The Times later described how the tragic events unfolded: 'The water rushed in with such extreme velocity, that the force of the air threw one man upon his back on the stage, and extinguished the gas. It is difficult to describe the agitation and alarm which prevailed among the workmen at this moment. Those who could get to the eastern arch effected their escape, and others were carried by the force of the water to the end of the shaft, and were taken out of the water in a state of extreme exhaustion. At one period about 18 men were all immersed in the water, besides Mr Brunel; and that gentleman and 12 of the men, after being repeatedly driven against the wood-work, and severely bruised, were taken out of the shaft nearly insensible.'

Brunel managed to escape the flooded tunnel, but some of his men did not. The two who had been working in the top compartment were killed almost instantly when the water broke through. Beneath them, their workmate Jephtha Cooke, who had been working in one of the bottom compartments, became trapped behind the rushing water and was drowned. George Evans, J. Long and W. Seton, all of whom had been working alongside Mr Cooke, also drowned when the tunnel exit collapsed.

The disaster almost spelled the end for the Brunels' ambitious project. Workmen were in fear for their lives; the existing part of the tunnel had sustained serious damage during the flood; funds were running out. Many investors now thought the project unworkable and morale among the workers reached an all-time low. Isambard Brunel, forced to take several weeks off to recuperate from his ordeal, found on his return that a massive amount of private investment in the project had been withdrawn.

No further work was done on the ill-fated tunnel for over five years, although the Brunels refused to give up on the scheme. Marc Brunel designed a new, improved tunnelling shield and, in 1834, his efforts paid off when he managed to secure funding to reopen the tunnel. Work began once again and gradually the shaft snaked its way under the Thames, finally emerging in Rotherhithe in November 1841, having cost nearly half a million pounds to build.

The Brunels had been lucky in securing investment for completion of the tunnel. When they asked for finance to build the ramps on which the horse-drawn wagons would descend, however, their investors' patience ran out. No further funding was supplied and the ramps were never built.

With no access for horses, the only way of entering the tunnel was via spiral staircases. The decision was therefore made that, instead of being used for cargo transportation, the tunnel would be opened to the public. Desperate to recoup some costs, the Brunels and the directors of the Thames Tunnel Company lost no time in promoting the tunnel. Even before it was completely finished, advertisements appeared in the *Illustrated London News*:

THE THAMES TUNNEL

Open to visitors daily (Sunday excepted), from 9am until 5pm and is brilliantly lighted with gas.
The entrance for a short time longer is only on the Middlesex side of the river, near the Tunnel Pier at Wapping, the Rotherhithe entrance being closed, in order to finish the new staircase.

The tunnel officially opened in the spring of 1843. To the Brunels' great relief, it was an instant success. On the opening day, it was reported that some 50,000 people walked through it, each paying a penny for the privilege. However, as the crowds gradually died down, the tunnel took on a more forbidding atmosphere, particularly at night. Thieves crouched in the shadows of the stairwells and its deeper recesses became a favourite spot for street prostitutes, who took customers there for a 'four-penny knee-trembler'.

As the years passed, the Thames Tunnel would be used less and less as its reputation declined. It seemed that the Brunels' troubled project was destined to become a white elephant, until the East London Railway expressed an interest in it in the early 1860s. The tunnel was subsequently sold to the railway company, which immediately laid tracks along its length. It reopened in 1869 as a goods railway, finally carrying freight from the docks to the national rail termini as Marc and Isambard Brunel had originally intended.

In the same year as the Thames Tunnel began a new life as a freight railway, a talented young engineer began building a second tunnel under the Thames using a method that was to revolutionise subterranean construction and spark a period of massive expansion under London's streets.

James Greathead was the son of an English merchant living in Grahamstown, a colonial outpost located on the remote Cape of Good Hope. By the time he was 16, his family had moved to Norfolk Villas, an elegant suburban terrace in Kensington, where he and his eight siblings continued their education. During his time at the exclusive Westbourne Collegiate School, Greathead showed both interest and flair in engineering. After his schooling was complete, he secured a sought-after position as apprentice to civil engineer Peter Barlow.

Barlow had been involved in several major railway construction projects prior to James Greathead's arrival, but probably his most important contribution to his profession would the ability to inspire his new pupil. Back in 1860, Barlow had been retained as engineer for the new Lambeth Bridge. In response to his brief, he created a majestic suspension bridge held in place amid the fast-flowing waters of the Thames by huge, hollow cast-iron piers driven deep into the riverbed. Barlow personally oversaw the construction of the project and, as he watched the great metal piers being sunk into the London clay, he realised the same process could be used to drive cylinders into the ground horizontally, thus creating a virtually indestructible tunnel encased in a metal tube.

Excited by his idea's potential, Barlow began to refine it. By 1867, he and his student Greathead had developed a proposal to build a network of underground

'Tube' railways inside which carriages would be propelled back and forth by cable traction. It secured royal assent and Barlow was able to try out the concept by building a subway under the Thames, linking Tower Hill with Vine Lane (off Tooley Street).

Keen to press ahead, Barlow placed advertisements inviting contractors to tender for this important project. To his dismay, he received no responses. The contractors had not forgotten the horrors of the Brunels' disastrous Thames Tunnel venture, and were not prepared to risk either their men or their finances on another ill-fated expedition below the river. Barlow was almost at the point of giving up the project when James Greathead (who at the time was just 24 years old) submitted his own tender to build the tunnel.

Greathead proposed using a modified and improved version of Marc Brunel's tunnelling shield. Circular in shape, Greathead's shield was reminiscent of a gigantic pastry cutter. It was driven into the tunnel face by jacks and was nearly 5ft deep, allowing men to work inside it with complete protection from collapsing earth or the sudden ingress of water.

Greathead quickly assembled a team to begin work on the Tower subway in early 1869. Amazingly, by December of the same year, the tunnel was finished. London's first 'Tube' railway would open in August 1870, but it soon transpired that Barlow's cable cars were not suitable for a long tunnel. The cables regularly broke, leaving passengers stranded and, even when it was working, the cars were interminably slow. After only weeks of service, the cable system was removed. Like its doomed predecessor, the Tower subway became a foot tunnel.

Although transport within the subway was ineffective, James Greathead's tunnelling shield proved revolutionary. Engineers and contractors were impressed by the speed and efficiency with which the subway had been created, and the government appreciated how underground tunnels could now be constructed without digging up the streets. However, the problem of how to run trains within the iron tubes remained.

Greathead continued to work on his tunnelling shield, making modifications and improvements while engaged on other engineering projects, all the time waiting for the opportunity to use it once again. In the meantime, his tunnel under the Thames languished. Despite the popularity of its method of crossing the river for dock workers and waterside labourers, its unavoidably claustrophobic atmosphere proved unpleasant to many visitors. The writer Edmondo de Amicis described the tunnel in his *Jottings about London* (1883):

'I went down and down between two dingy walls until I found myself at the opening of a gigantic iron tube, which seemed to undulate like a great intestine in the enormous belly of the river. The inside of this tube presents the appearance of a subterranean corridor, of which the end is invisible. It is lighted by a row of lights as far as you can see, which shed veiled light, like sepulchral lamps; the atmosphere is foggy; you go along considerable stretches without meeting a soul; the walls are like those of an aqueduct; the floor moves under your feet like the deck of a vessel; the steps and voices of the people coming the other way give forth a cavernous sound, and are heard before you see the people, and they at a distance seem like great shadows; there is in short, a sort of something mysterious, which without alarming, causes in your heart a vague sense of disquiet.'

The Tower subway continued as a foot tunnel until 1894, when the completion of Tower Bridge gave Londoners a more pleasant (and gratis) method of traversing the Thames. It was subsequently sold off to a company whose pipes were occupying an increasing amount of space beneath the city streets – the London Hydraulic Power Company.

The concept of hydraulic power had been explored earlier in the century, when a wealthy industrialist named William Armstrong used water pressure to power a quayside crane in Newcastle. Impressed with the efficiency of the system and thinking ahead of his time, Armstrong became an energetic promoter of renewable energy, volubly eschewing the use of coal in favour of machinery operated either by water pressure or solar power.

The owners of London's docks became intrigued by how Armstrong's hydraulically powered cranes operated in the north-east of England. In 1871, the verbosely titled Wharves and Warehouses Steam Power and Hydraulic Pressure Company was formed, with a view to laying a network of cast-iron underground hydraulic pipes along the banks of the Thames in east London, to power the heavy lifting machinery employed in the docks.

This new form of power proved a success, as it quickly became clear that hydraulic pressure was efficient and cost-effective in comparison with gas or coal, if used to power intermittently operated machinery. Consequently, the Hydraulic Pressure Company was employed to drive machinery as diverse as industrial coffee grinders, ventilation systems, elevators and crushing machines. In 1884, the firm changed its name to the less-unwieldy London Hydraulic Power Company. By 1890, it had laid over 40 miles of pipes under the metropolis from the East End to Victoria. These robust cast-iron channels were soon joined by underground conduits constructed by another 19th-century energy supplier.

Back in 1876, wealthy baronet Sir Coutts Lindsay had decided to indulge his passion for art by building a picture gallery on New Bond Street. He named it the Grosvenor Gallery and its first exhibition opened, to much acclaim, in May 1877.

Although the gallery was an instant success, personal financial problems meant that Lindsay was constantly investigating ways to increase visitor receipts. Over the years following its opening, he installed a restaurant, a library and then, in 1883, decided to illuminate his collections with the very latest technological innovation – electric light.

In order to achieve this, Lindsay built a generator on land at the back of his gallery and ran cables to the exhibits along the walls of the building. The results were astounding. Visitors were now able to view the paintings at any time of day, without having them spoiled by the flickering flame of gaslights. In fact, the electric lights themselves became novel exhibits. As patrons flocked to the gallery, the canny shopkeepers on New Bond Street asked Lindsay if he might light their premises in return for an annual fee. Realising that he could make a small fortune, Lindsay agreed and proceeded to build a larger generator in the gallery's basement.

At first, the Grosvenor Gallery generator supplied its customers via overhead cables that ran along the rooftops. That was until the appointment of electrical engineer Sebastian Ziani de Ferranti, who improved the reliability of the power supply by relocating the cables underground, where they would remain. By this time, demand was so great that Lindsay felt compelled to form the London Electricity Supply Corporation – the capital's first electricity company.

In 1890, lack of space at the gallery prompted Lindsay and de Ferranti to build a new purpose-built generating station at Deptford. (The original site of the Grosvenor Gallery became a substation, a modernised version of which can still be found at the same address today.) The Deptford power station proved to be a huge success and, by 1900, numerous electricity companies were springing up all over London. As more and more of the capital got connected, so the underground network of electricity cables expanded proportionately.

By this time, the collection of pipes, cables and tunnels under London was becoming labyrinthine. However, developing the city below ground had two major factors in its favour: unsightly cables, sewers and pipelines were hidden from the public gaze and virtually immune to vandalism; the vast space beneath the city also meant that, despite the regular introduction of new utilities and the extension of existing networks, there was still plenty of room.

This fact did not pass unnoticed by the railway companies. During the latter part of the 19th century, London's population exploded as the city played host to waves of immigrants from a range of countries as far flung as Ireland and Russia. With this increase in population came a rise in demand for food and housing, as the railways' goods depots overflowed with produce and building materials. In a bid to solve the problem, the railway companies looked underground.

In north London, a subterranean distribution network was built that connected Euston mainline station with the large goods depot at Chalk Farm. Deep beneath the bustling streets, horses pulled wagons laden with goods through a series of crypt-like tunnels and chambers leading to several distribution points. From Euston, the tunnel meandered through the southern part of Camden Town towards Primrose Hill. Here it met with a subterranean canal basin in which goods could be transferred onto barges and taken into the City via the Regent's Canal. The underground tunnels then led to a series of warehouses buried under the Camden Town goods depot, sandwiched between Gloucester Avenue and Chalk Farm Road (the site of today's Camden Market). Once at the depot, the goods could be hauled up to ground level and loaded onto the trains of the London & North Western or North London Railways.

Around the same time as the Camden Town tunnels were built, another subterranean railway warehouse was being constructed further east, underneath Bishopsgate railway station. Bishopsgate started life in the 1840s as the terminus of the Eastern Counties Railway. However, in 1862 the company merged with other lines to form the Great Eastern Railway and, by the mid-1870s, the terminus was moved to nearby Liverpool Street. Although Bishopsgate's low-level passenger platforms (situated on the opposite side of Commercial Street) continued to be used, the main part of the station fell into disuse and the last train departed in 1879.

Bishopsgate outlived its usefulness as a passenger terminus, but it was in a prime location with good transport links. The Great Eastern's goods depot at Brick Lane was rapidly becoming too small to cope with the huge amount of goods arriving there, and so the railway company developed a new freight depot on the site. Work began at the end of 1879 and two years later Bishopsgate goods station opened.

The new structure was an impressive sight. A huge iron and glass roof supported by rows of sturdy ferrous columns covered the tracks, themselves flanked by lines of platforms. This is where trucks were unloaded and goods sent down under the station to a vast warehouse divided into a series of tunnel vaults. Vehicle access to this underground basement was via a series of ramps leading from the surrounding streets.

The Great Eastern had originally intended its subterranean warehouse to house a new fresh produce market. Indeed, in December 1881, *The Times* had reported: 'The Great Eastern Railway Company are now constructing an extensive fish, fruit and vegetable market underneath their new goods depot … The area set apart for the purpose is about four and a half acres. Three lines of rails will be laid down the centre of the plot, to which trucks will be lowered by hydraulic hoists from the goods station above. On the north will be a row of 38 warehouses for fish, and on the south 16 large warehouses for fruit and vegetables, each having a cellar beneath and offices … The market will have four entrances, two from Brick Lane, one from Bethnal Green Road and one from Norton Folgate.'

Unfortunately for the Great Eastern, its proposal for a new fruit and vegetable market was energetically contested by the owner of Spitalfields Market, situated only a five-minute walk away. The courts ruled in his favour and Bishopsgate station's underground market would never come to pass. Nevertheless, its underground warehouse was put to full use. By the 1930s, the goods depot would employ nearly 1,500 staff and handle up to 3,000 tons of produce per day.

CHAPTER 5

THE TRANSPORT BOOM

Although the land beneath the north side of the Thames had been effectively used to transport both people and goods, men and women living in the suburbs of south London still had a difficult time commuting into the City to work.

The London, Chatham & Dover Railway had provided a means of getting into the capital for commuters south of the Thames since 1859, but those using the line were faced with two problems. Firstly, the trains were massively overcrowded, which made for an exceedingly unpleasant journey during the rush hour; secondly, the trains terminated at Blackfriars which, although on the north side of the river, was a fair distance from the heart of the City. In bad weather, commuters faced the misery of enduring cramped conditions on the train, followed by a cold, wet trek on foot to their place of work. The alternative was to take an omnibus from Blackfriars station, but this method of transport was expensive and slow. As Londoner Arthur Beavan noted in his book *Up-To-Date Locomotion* (1903):

'At the close of business, men of all ranks want to get home as fast as they can, and from some station not far from their counting houses ... how could any of those gentlemen clad in irreproachable frock coats and new, glossy hats, who each day of the week issued from snug offices in Austin Friars, Drapers' Gardens or Copthall Court ... if resident on the Surrey side, be expected to go to and from business by way of Blackfriars?'

The concept of a new underground railway linking south London to the City inspired James Greathead, who had been waiting some time for another opportunity to use his tunnelling shield. Aided by John Fowler and his assistant Benjamin Baker, Greathead drew up an ambitious scheme for a subterranean railway with twin tunnels, running from the Elephant & Castle under the Thames to King William Street in the heart of the City, with trains propelled by a much improved version of the previously disastrous cable traction system. The proposal was not met with enthusiasm. Detractors argued that all previous attempts to run a railway under the Thames had ended in abject failure, and that the last thing London needed was another costly foot tunnel.

Undeterred, Greathead and his fellow engineers argued that advances in engineering had made underground cable traction a much more viable proposition and that, more importantly, their new line would have a dramatic effect on the overcrowded trains and severe gridlock suffered every weekday on thoroughfares leading into the City. Their tireless campaigning eventually paid off. On 28 July 1884, the City of London & Southwark Subway Company was incorporated, with James Greathead as chief engineer and Fowler and Baker acting as consultants.

Greathead's original plan was for twin underground tunnels running from the terminus at the Elephant & Castle, through the Borough to London Bridge, where they would descend beneath the bed of the river and the streets of the City to the northern terminus at the junction of King William and Arthur Streets. Work began in October 1886 and, by the following year, confidence in the previously derided project had grown to such an extent that the company secured permission to extend the line southwards through Kennington and Stockwell. The only doubtful part of the scheme was the use of cable-driven trains, but this was soon to change.

As work on the tunnels progressed, improvements in the use of electrical power led the directors to consider it as the driving force for their railway. They watched with interest as the Metropolitan Railway conducted experiments with electrically powered locomotives and thus began their own trials. The prospect of the new subterranean line being powered by electricity was exciting to investors and so, in 1889, the engineering firm of Mather & Platt were awarded the contract for electrifying the line and designing the locomotives and carriages.

Initially, 14 locomotives were built and painted in a smart, rust-coloured livery. The construction of the carriages was contracted out to the Ashbury Railway Carriage & Iron Company of Openshaw, near Manchester, and their unique design caused much debate. Commonly referred to as 'padded cells', the carriages took the form of a domed box on wheels. Access to the enclosed, airless compartments was via an open platform at the end of each car, across which stretched lattice-framed gates similar to those used on hydraulic lifts. These gates were opened by guards each time the train rolled into a station.

Once inside the carriages, passengers were met with a dark compartment, dimly lit by four electric lights mounted in the ceiling and flanked by rows of seating upholstered in heavy padded fabric, studded with buttons. The upholstery extended almost to the carriage ceiling, interrupted only by rows of tiny windows that afforded no view whatsoever, giving an atmosphere that might charitably be described as cosy but in reality was probably more than a little claustrophobic.

The world's first electrically powered 'Tube' line – now known as the City & South London Railway – opened on 4 November 1890. It sparked a revolution in public transport. Although the 'padded cell' cars were not to everyone's liking, passengers could at least enjoy a quiet, smoke-free journey. Patrons of the City & South London Railway also benefited from a wonderfully simple ticketing system. Gone were the options of first-, second- or third-class fares, along with the confusing array of season passes. As *The Times* noted on the opening day:

'The new railway will have a single class and a single fare. The intending passenger will simply put down 2d., and pass through a turnstile. He is then free of the place. He enters a lift, is carried down 50 feet to the station platform, gets into the next train in whichever direction he chooses, travels to the next station, or to the next but one, or to the terminus as he thinks fit, and then is finally brought back by hydraulic power to the upper air once more.'

London's expanding underground railway was gradually distancing itself from its overground forebears, becoming a separate entity with its own unique operating system.

The construction of the City & South London Tube proved to the sceptical that it was now possible to build cost-effective railway lines under the Thames. The commuters of south London had their journey times cut in half by this new, cheap and convenient service. It was therefore unsurprising that other underground railway schemes attracted a lot of interest from investors, particularly one that connected the City to the mainline terminus of the London & South Western Railway at Waterloo.

Although the station had dominated the area since the late 1840s, it had always been out on a limb as there was no onward connection to either the West End or the City. The success of the City & South London line prompted directors of the London & South Western to approach James Greathead with a view to running a new line under the City from their overground terminal to the Mansion House, close to the Bank of England.

Greathead agreed to take on the role of consulting engineer for the project, working alongside the London & South Western's resident engineer, William Galbraith. The men were ably assisted by Galbraith's colleague Harley Dalrymple-Hay, who would spend much of his working life enlarging London's Tube network as well as creating private subterranean passageways such as the Harrods tunnel, which ran under the Brompton Road to a warehouse on the south side of what is today Trevor Square.

By 1893, Greathead and his eminent colleagues had been given the go-ahead to construct a twin-tunnel subterranean railway running from Waterloo station to the City, with work commencing a year later. The tunnels followed a route that ran beneath Stamford Street before turning diagonally under the Thames toward the northern foot of Blackfriars Bridge, travelling into the City under Queen Victoria Street to a terminus at the Mansion House (now known as Bank station).

Greathead's considerable experience came to the fore during construction, which took just three years to complete. Once again, the efficiency of his great tunnelling shield astounded those who witnessed its progress across the City. At the official opening of the new Waterloo & City Line, in July 1898, as guest of honour, HRH The Duke of Cambridge observed, 'If, 60 years ago, anybody had ventured to predict that London was likely to see such a railway, he would have been considered a fit subject for a lunatic asylum.' That 'such a railway' was now a reality was largely due to James Greathead.

Luckily for the companies involved, the construction of both the City & South London and Waterloo & City Railways had not met much resistance from the general public. Most Londoners had surmised that the benefits of improved transport outweighed the inconvenience – although the next underground railway proposal was not embraced so readily.

As the City & South London line was nearing completion, a Bill for a Central London Railway was heard in the House of Commons, causing a great deal of controversy. The major problem with the proposed underground line was its route, connecting west London with the City by starting at a terminus near Paddington station, then running through the West End and Holborn to terminate at Mansion House. This provided the perfect route to travel between the two great cities of London and Westminster, but there were two main points of contention. The District Railway energetically opposed the scheme, fearing it would poach custom from their own lines, but the major cause for concern was that construction would entail digging up a large portion of Oxford Street, London's main retail thoroughfare, causing huge losses in sales.

In December 1889, the tradesmen and residents of Oxford Street met at Marylebone Court House to air their collective fears regarding the new railway. One Mr Blackburn, representing silversmiths Mappin & Webb (whose flagship store was at 77-78 Oxford Street), opened by declaring, 'this meeting of the inhabitants of Oxford Street condemns the proposal to construct any subway or railway under the street, believing that the obstruction to the traffic during the construction … would entail most serious losses to all persons along the line of the route [and] that such a subway is not required for public convenience'.

Mr Blackburn's motion was quickly seconded by Mr Gotto of Oxford Street stationers Parkins & Gotto, and a committee was formed to block the railway proposal. Mr Goddard of the Peter Robinson firm of drapers suggested that all Oxford Street stores should contribute to a defence fund.

Oxford Street retailers were not alone in opposing the scheme. Soon they were joined by the Marylebone Vestry and the Bishop of London himself, who publicly voiced his concern that the City section of the new line would jeopardise the foundations of St Paul's Cathedral. This proved too much for the government and the Bill was rejected by the House of Lords.

Undeterred, advocates of the Central London Railway concluded that if they could make the line more useful to the general public, the somewhat unfounded reservations of retailers and the guardians of St Paul's could be ignored. In a bold move, they extended the route westwards to Shepherd's Bush, arguing that the line would now provide easy access to central London for literally thousands more commuters, thus increasing footfall in the retail districts. Their strategy worked. In August 1891, Parliament approved their plan for a new underground railway running from a terminus at Shepherd's Bush, through the affluent suburbs of Notting Hill and Westbourne Grove to Oxford Street, thence into the City via Bloomsbury, Holborn and Newgate Street. One year later, further approval was given to extend the line to Liverpool Street, where it would connect with trains taking City workers out to their homes in the suburbs of east London and Essex.

Preparatory work on the line began as soon as the scheme received royal assent. James Greathead, John Fowler (who had been knighted for his services to engineering in 1890) and their old colleague Benjamin Baker were retained as chief engineers. It was hoped that with such experienced men overseeing the project, progress would be swift. As soon as the scheme got underway, however, the proposed site of the Shepherd's Bush terminus began to stir up more trouble.

The land selected for the Central London Railway's west London terminus was occupied by an old estate known as Woodhouse Park. Its owners, a consortium called the Kensington Woodhouse Park Syndicate, demanded a massive £32,790 for their land, claiming the park was ideally situated for exhibitions and therefore worth a lot of money to them.

Indeed, the popularity of exhibitions in London had been gradually gaining momentum since the Great Exhibition of 1851. However, the staging of these events was a hit and miss affair, and the railway's directors argued that, contrary to the syndicate's claims, west London was a totally inappropriate site for exhibitions. At the subsequent Sheriff's Court hearing they brought in Mr A. Johnstone, accountant for the nearby Earl's Court Exhibitions Company, who lamented how Buffalo Bill's Wild West Show of 1887 had made a catastrophic loss of £70,000 for his firm, their 'Italian Exhibition' trade show the following year had lost £8,000 and its recent German counterpart had produced a deficit of £25,000. Mr Johnstone's damning figures were backed by exhibition organiser Mr J. Hart, who declared Woodhouse Park 'wholly unsuitable for the purposes of an exhibition'. With no evidence to support their counter argument, the syndicate were forced to concede and eventually sold Woodhouse Park to the Central London Railway for just £5,000.

Although the company had succeeded in obtaining the land for their western terminus at a fair price, the court case held up the works considerably. Further disputes over compensation with property owners in the densely packed districts of Marylebone and the City delayed proceedings even further. Then, in 1896, just as the company was finally at the stage of employing a works contractor, it suffered probably its most affecting setback.

Not long after he was appointed consultant engineer to the Central London Railway, James Greathead had fallen ill with severe gastric problems, later diagnosed as the effects of stomach cancer. With no drug therapy available at the time, his doctors advised that the only course of action was to operate and attempt to cut the cancer out of his system. Greathead survived the operation, but, while convalescing, suddenly collapsed and died at his home in Streatham on 21 October 1896, aged just 52.

Despite his untimely death, Greathead's engineering genius lived on through his greatest achievement. The tunnelling shield that bore his name created the Central London Railway's tunnels with such speed that by 1898, they were almost complete. The original line ran from Shepherd's Bush to the Mansion House, as the company decided to complete the extension to Liverpool

Street as a separate scheme once the main line was open. In between the two termini lay 11 stations: Holland Park, Notting Hill Gate, Queens Road (today's Queensway), Westbourne Park, Marble Arch, Davies Street (near Bond Street, which later lent the station its name), Oxford Circus, Tottenham Court Road, British Museum, Chancery Lane and General Post Office (now St Paul's). The line was set to revolutionise travel across central London, with the company predicting that once the extension to Liverpool Street was completed, it would take just 25 minutes to journey from one end of the line to the other. (At the time, the same journey by omnibus took over an hour.)

As carpenters, joiners and other craftsmen made the finishing touches to the Central London Railway, the project was once again overshadowed by death. At the end of 1898, Sir John Fowler, who was now 81 and had been suffering ill-health for some time, collapsed and died at his home in Bournemouth. By the time the railway was officially opened in June 1900, Benjamin Baker was the company's last surviving consultant engineer.

Nonetheless, the monumental achievements and pioneering vision of Greathead and Fowler would withstand the test of time. The tunnels they created at the end of the 19th century would not only transform public transport in the capital but also set the template for underground railway systems across Europe and beyond. In the years that followed the opening of the Central London Railway, Greathead and Fowler's engineering methods would be used to create the Great Northern & City Railway – which took GNR trains under the streets of Finsbury Park, Islington and Old Street to a terminus at Moorgate – and the Baker Street & Waterloo Railway (otherwise known as the Bakerloo Line), which opened in 1906 (as did the Piccadilly Line).

By 1908, London had eight railways that ran beneath the heart of the city. The Bakerloo Line connected Edgware Road in the north with Elephant & Castle in the south. The Central London Railway ran from Shepherd's Bush to the Bank of England. The City & South London Railway connected Euston mainline station with the leafy suburbs of Clapham Common. The old Metropolitan Railway spread beyond the confines of central London, emerging from dark tunnels to convey passengers above ground to far-flung semi-rural suburbs such as Harrow, Putney and Rickmansworth. Over in the east, the District Line snaked its way through the industrial communities of Bow, Bromley and East Ham. Further west, the Piccadilly Railway ran from Finsbury Park in the north to Hammersmith via the West End, with a connection at Leicester Square for the Hampstead Railway. The latter line also split in two at Camden Town, taking passengers further north to termini at Golders Green and Highgate, where omnibuses and electric trams conveyed them even further away to the sleepy backwaters of Finchley and Barnet.

By the end of the 19th century, Charles Pearson's dream of Londoners escaping the crowded city centre had become reality. Families once forced to live in the densely packed streets of Whitechapel, Paddington, Islington or the Borough moved out to the open spaces of Holloway, Willesden or Clapham, paying just tuppence to travel into town. The inspiration of the great railway engineers had combined with the strength and expertise of thousands of navvies, labourers and artisans, sparking a transport revolution that changed the social geography of the city.

✍

Although the tentacles of the underground railways began to stretch across the whole of London, one area remained virtually untouched: the Port of London stretched from the St Katharine Docks, close to the Tower, south-eastwards along the Thames to Woolwich. In between lay massive enclosed docks and hundreds of smaller wharves, all of which dealt with tons of cargo every day. Prior to the 1890s, however, this bustling, heavily populated part of the capital had no crossings over the River Thames, bar a smattering of ferry services. Consequently, roads leading to the nearest crossing, at London Bridge, were constantly jammed with carriages and carts.

Residents and business owners in east London constantly complained about the local transport infrastructure and eventually, after much deliberation, Parliament bowed to pressure. In 1885, the Corporation of London obtained authorisation to build Tower Bridge. Two years later, the Metropolitan Board of Works gained permission to build an underground river crossing for both pedestrians and vehicles between the ancient maritime districts of Blackwall and Greenwich. Anxious to begin the project, they asked their long-standing engineer Joseph Bazalgette to design the new river crossing. In response, Bazalgette drew up plans for two tunnels – one for vehicles and the other for pedestrians – and began calculating the cost of the project. However, in this instance Bazalgette's vision would never materialise. In March 1889, the Metropolitan Board of Works was replaced by the newly formed London County Council and responsibility for the new Thames tunnel was handed over to the LCC's engineer-in-chief, Alexander Binnie.

Although he had been born in Ladbroke Grove, Binnie spent much of his working life away from London on projects in Wales and, later, India. He did, however, maintain a keen interest in the pioneering work on the capital's underground railways and, once commissioned to design the LCC's new subaqueous tunnel, lost no time in consulting railway engineers as to the best way forward.

After much discussion with Greathead, Fowler and Baker, Binnie decided to construct the new river crossing using the same engineering principles applied to the City & South London Railway tunnels. He also calculated that costs could be kept to a minimum by dispensing with Bazalgette's foot tunnel, instead laying pavements for unfortunate pedestrians inside the road tunnel, where they would have to endure the noise and stench of horse-drawn carts as they made their way under the river. The resulting blueprint was a plan for the largest subaqueous tunnel in the world, over 6,000ft long with a diameter of 27ft, running from the East India Dock Road at Blackwall to the Woolwich Road on the south side of the river. The tunnel would be dug using a revised version of Greathead's shield and its interior lined with iron cylinders faced with glazed brickwork. Brave pedestrians would be able to access it from spiral staircases with domed glass roofs.

By 1891, Binnie's plans were approved by the LCC. The job was put out to tender and the contract awarded to Samuel Pearson & Son, a family firm from Yorkshire which would become the huge media conglomerate Pearson plc in later years. As building work commenced in early 1892, it soon became apparent that Pearson's men were faced with a tricky task. In addition to driving the largest underwater tunnel ever attempted through solid clay, the route of the tunnel was so confined – due to its proximity to numerous docks and wharves – that in some sections workmen were forced to dig dangerously close to the riverbed. In order to avoid a repeat of the disasters that occurred in Brunel's Thames Tunnel decades previously, compressed air was employed to keep the roof in place. Fearful of the effect this might have on his workers, Binnie cautiously arranged compensation for any man killed or injured as a result.

In the event, Binnie's compensation scheme was not needed. Work progressed swiftly and, on 30 October 1895, the tunnel was in a sufficiently complete state for the contractor to organise the now obligatory subterranean banquet for local dignitaries. As *The Times* reported:

'Messrs Pearson have accomplished what promised to be by far the most difficult part of the undertaking. On this they may well be congratulated, as well as on the immunity from fatal accidents which they have enjoyed.

No workman has been killed either by falling off scaffolds (for which the two deep shafts at each end afford ample opportunity) or by mishaps from the machinery; nor has there been any death from the effects of compressed air. This is no doubt due to the care with which the men were medically examined before being allowed to work under the high pressures which were at times necessary.'

On the weekend following the banquet, the contractor opened the tunnel to the public to achieve more publicity for his high-profile project. On payment of 3d, interested parties were given a tour of the works by Poplar councillor Will Crooks – a man who was to become instrumental in further subaqueous tunnelling for east London.

The Blackwall Tunnel finally opened to traffic in May 1897 and was an immediate success. In true Victorian fashion, it was not merely functional. Each end of the tunnel was guarded by a majestic stone gatehouse. Vehicles passed beneath a high arch in the centre of the buildings, flanked by four capped turrets. The imposing northern gatehouse provided accommodation for the tunnel caretaker: above its central arch lay two bedrooms, a parlour, a larder and scullery and a WC, with a third bedroom created in the roof. The two elaborate gatehouses had a rather incongruous impact on the local landscape. As editor Hermione Hobhouse noted in the *Survey of London Volumes 43 and 44: Poplar, Blackwall and Isle of Dogs* (1994): 'The gatehouses provided unusual Art Nouveau silhouettes amid the working class housing of Poplar and the empty expanses and gas storage tanks for Greenwich marshes.'

The arrival of the Blackwall Tunnel coincided with interesting times in east London. During the 1890s, the docks – which dominated the area both geographically and financially – became increasingly unionised as the workers realised that, collectively, they wielded a surprising amount of power. The residents of Poplar and Greenwich welcomed the new free route across the Thames, while dockers working at the Millwall and Surrey Commercial Docks found the tunnel of little use, as it was too far away from their place of work. They were forced to continue using the ferryboats to take them across the river, but these craft were notoriously unreliable, especially during inclement weather. While the majority of dock workers contented themselves with merely complaining to one another about their terrible journeys back and forth across the Thames, a few took it upon themselves to resolve the problem. One such man was Will Crooks, a cooper from Poplar who actively supported the embryonic Labour movement.

Crooks was born in 1852 in Shirbutt Street, Poplar, close to the massive West India Docks. His father George worked at the Port of London as a ship's stoker but, while Will was still very young, his father was involved in a horrendous accident which resulted in the amputation of his right arm. Unable to work at his previous employment, George was forced to scratch around for menial jobs and the family quickly sank into chronic poverty that ultimately led to the workhouse.

At the age of 14, Will Crooks secured regular work as an apprentice cooper, but his tough (indeed at times destitute) upbringing drove him to encourage his fellow workers to stand up to exploitation by their employers via one of the new trades unions. In order to get his message across, Crooks tutored himself in the art of public speaking and gained invaluable experience by delivering lectures outside the gates of the East India Dock every Sunday morning.

Soon after the London County Council was created, Crooks was elected council member for Poplar and immediately used his new position to improve the neighbourhood that he represented. Will Crooks' campaigns were manifold and encompassed all manner of social problems, from poor housing to caring for the sick. However, one of his most popular crusades was to create new foot tunnels for dockworkers underneath the Thames. When he was appointed chairman of the Council's bridges committee in 1898, Crooks saw the chance to turn this idea into a reality.

Following his spirited campaign, the LCC gained approval for the construction of a foot tunnel to run from the southern tip of the Isle of Dogs to Greenwich, with the contractors Cochrane & Co beginning work in June 1899. Less than two years later, the tunnel was opened with a surprising lack of ceremony. Although the completion of the Greenwich Foot Tunnel (as it became known) passed with little comment it proved an absolute boon to local dockworkers, who now had a free and fast way of crossing the Thames whatever the weather. The tunnel itself was an unassuming affair, measuring just over 1,200ft in length. At its deepest point, it lay 72ft beneath ground level; its simple interior was clad in glossy white tiles designed to reflect the dim electric light running along the uppermost curve of the roof; at either end of the tunnel, lifts and a staircase led pedestrians back above ground via attractive, circular redbrick entranceways with elegant domed glass roofs.

The new foot tunnel proved so popular that Will Crooks and his colleagues began to press for a second, this time connecting North and South Woolwich. As had been the case on the Isle of Dogs, anyone crossing the Thames to work at the Royal Docks was constantly let down by the Woolwich ferry service, especially when it was foggy. The success of the Greenwich Foot Tunnel made the campaigners' task relatively easy and, by October 1912, the new Woolwich Foot Tunnel was open, running 60ft beneath the old undependable ferry crossing.

The instant success of the Blackwall, Greenwich and Woolwich tunnels, and their dramatic effect on Port of London morale and distribution of cargoes, prompted the construction of a fourth tunnel in east London. In 1904, work began on the Rotherhithe Tunnel, running nearly 7,000ft under the river from Lower Road, Rotherhithe to Commercial Street, Stepney. Unfortunately, its construction necessitated the destruction of an ancient part of maritime London.

On the north side of the river, the clearances required for the construction of the Rotherhithe Tunnel approach destroyed little that was worth keeping. This part of the East End had long since descended into iniquity. Many of the rougher streets had been cleared during the early 1890s, but those that remained were lined with cheap lodgings occupied by 'sailors' widows' – a polite euphemism for prostitutes. One block away from the Thames lay Medland Street, a partially demolished, derelict road that was a favourite resort of local itinerants due to Medland Hall, a cheap lodging house connected to the Congregational Union church. In 1914, a *Times* journalist visited the hall (which had survived the tunnel clearance) and described the abject sleeping accommodation:

'Recently, under the London County Council's regulations prescribing a minimum of 350 cu ft of air space for every bed, the accommodation at Medland Hall has been reduced, and now about 180 beds a night are occupied. They are real beds; but they are only just raised above the floor, each in a wooden box frame, and as one passes among them in the dim light, the oblong boxes scattered about the floors, each with its motionless human figure within, are gruesomely suggestive. Most of the occupants lie in restful attitudes and sleep soundly. But here one has thrust his covering down below the waist and lies cramped and huddled. Another tosses and mutters, with arms thrown above the head. It is not ideally comfortable or luxurious. But it is a bed, and quiet and shelter for the night; and it costs nothing. It is not a little thing to give a chance of peaceful sleep with warmth and shelter to something like 200 homeless people every night.'

While the streets surrounding the northern entrance of the Rotherhithe Tunnel possessed a poverty-stricken air, those near the works at Rotherhithe had a wholly different atmosphere. This peninsula on the bank of the Thames had an old maritime feel to it. The nearby Surrey Commercial Docks still dealt with the elegant sailing ships that were rapidly being replaced by steam-driven vessels, their tall masts often visible over the terraced rooftops of nearby dockworkers' cottages.

The area was a popular place to live. In addition to the regular work on the docks and the related industries that operated close by, the living accommodation was eminently preferable to that on the opposite bank of the river. Most of the houses, while small, had their own gardens; rents were comparatively low; the City was easily accessible via Tower Bridge. In addition, the massive dock complex and Southwark Park gave the area a spacious open feel that was simply unknown in other areas. Many mourned the loss of the neat terraces that had to be demolished to make way for the tunnel's southern approach, but few disputed that the new river crossing would benefit the area.

The tunnel had been designed by Maurice Fitzmaurice, an ex-apprentice of Benjamin Baker who, after working for the LCC since 1892, became its chief engineer in 1901. The contractor chosen for the job was the firm of Price & Reeves, who got on with the task quickly, finishing 16 months ahead of schedule. The resulting tunnel was, at the time, the largest ever driven using the Greathead shield system. To mark this achievement, the outer cutting ring of the shield was sliced in half and used as a triumphal arch over the tunnel entrances.

The tunnel was opened in 1908 by the Prince of Wales, and was immediately acclaimed a success. In the early hours of the morning, hundreds of casual workers used it to cross the river in search of work at the docks. Later, cargoes from the majestic ships berthed in the dock basins were loaded onto carts and transported through the tunnel to the centre of the City, or to the mainline railway stations. From the outset, over 2,500 vehicles passed through the Rotherhithe Tunnel every day, justifying both the cost and the disruption.

The subaqueous tunnels in east London transformed the working lives of thousands of people employed at the Port of London. However, as the dockers made their way to work via new tunnels under the Thames, dark clouds were gathering that were to temporarily change the nature of London's subterranean labyrinth.

CHAPTER 6

WARTIME UNDERGROUND

D uring the summer of 1913, an innovative scheme was approved to revolutionise the way in which parcels and letters were transported across London. Its exponents planned to build a subterranean Post Office Railway, running from the Royal Mail's District Office at Paddington, under the West End and Holborn, to the main sorting office at Mount Pleasant. From there it would continue east into the City, terminating at Liverpool Street mainline train station.

Despite a degree of scepticism from some Post Office employees, aware of how the Pneumatic Despatch Company's attempt at running underground mail between Euston station and Eversholt Street in the 1860s/70s had proven slow and inefficient, the project was welcomed on the whole. Work on the scheme began in early 1914, with James Greathead's old colleague Harley Dalrymple-Hay acting as chief engineer. However, within just a few months construction of the Post Office Railway ground to a halt, as longstanding tensions in Europe erupted into war.

As soon as Britain entered the conflict in early August 1914, the atmosphere in London abruptly changed – both above and below ground. One contemporary journalist observed how the City became full of soldiers: 'Long lines of whistling, singing khaki tramp down Oxford-street or Piccadilly. The parks are full of drilling khaki … trench making is practised behind Westminster Cathedral … guns may be seen trundling down the quiet roads of St John's Wood; and in the Inns of Court, the big open squares of Bloomsbury, in every large open space the shout of the Sergeant Instructor may be heard.'

Underneath the city streets, Tube carriages filled up with excited young men on their way to the battlefields. As an increasing number left London, building works throughout the capital ground to a halt. At the Post Office Railway site, Dalrymple-Hay was faced with the impossible task of constructing a subterranean tunnel with a rapidly decreasing pool of labour. The project hobbled along for some months as the contractor desperately searched for men fit enough to undertake backbreaking work. Despite the best efforts of all involved, work on the new underground railway was finally forced to a halt in the closing months of 1915, when the government requisitioned most of the material used to create the tunnel lining and tracks for much-needed munitions. Although the unfinished railway was not fit for its original purpose, it did find an unexpected use.

In January 1915, a Zeppelin airship appeared over the British coastline, dropping powerful bombs on the seaside towns of King's Lynn and Great Yarmouth. Over the ensuing months more German airships arrived, each time edging closer to London. Soon, the city would come under attack from the skies; on 31 May, nearly 100 bombs fell on the capital.

Although the number of casualties was mercifully small, the city's institutions were thrown into panic. Museums, libraries and galleries realised that their priceless collections could go up in smoke at any time and sought places in which to store their most precious artefacts. The unfinished Post Office Railway became the unlikely repository for an eclectic assortment of relics. Ancient documents from the Public Record Office sat alongside old masters from the Tate and National Portrait Galleries. The terminus at Paddington became a temporary storage site for the Wallace Collection's artworks. Even mummies from the British Museum were temporarily entombed within the subterranean tunnel.

The Post Office Railway was not the only underground site to be commandeered as a bomb shelter. Aldwych Tube station was converted into a bunker for the War Office. It was also rumoured that the Royal Family sought sanctuary from the air raids by boarding the Royal Train, which was then shunted into an unspecified deep-level railway tunnel. Close by, thousands of ordinary Londoners sought their own refuge in nearby Tube stations.

At first, the use of Underground stations as shelters was unregulated. When local church bells rang out their warning of approaching aircraft, special constables, railway staff and even boy scouts assembled at the station entrances to ensure all those seeking shelter went down to the platforms in a safe and orderly fashion. Many refugees then took trains far out into the suburbs, where they would remain until the bombing had ceased; others stayed on the platforms. Once down in the congested makeshift refuges, the only source of food was the vending machines mounted on the platform walls, which some enterprising youths took advantage of. As soon as the air-raid warning was raised, they would rush down the stairs and quickly empty the machines, reselling the contents at hugely inflated prices to their hungry fellow refugees.

London's Underground stations soon developed a reputation as both convenient and effective air-raid shelters. Despite obvious safety issues incurred by hundreds of people in close proximity to unprotected live rails, accidents were mercifully rare.

The bombing raids of World War 1 were the first time that London was subjected to airborne assaults. As Londoners sheltered in the Tube stations while enemy bombs demolished their homes and wrecked their businesses, they could hardly have anticipated how, in just over 20 years' time, they would come under a more sustained attack.

In the aftermath of the Great War, few people thought far ahead. They concentrated on rebuilding their lives, following the destruction and loss that seemed to touch every inhabitant of the city. Suspended projects such as the Post Office Railway were resumed, but now the mood was very different. Hundreds of the contractors' workmen lay dead in ravaged fields across the Channel. When they died, they took with them the last vestiges of the Victorian entrepreneurial spirit that built underground London. The concept that 'anything is possible', so beloved of the great 19th-century engineers, lay buried in the bloodied mud of Ypres, Mons and the Somme.

The underground projects that took place after 1918 were rooted in necessity. Munitions work in factories during the war had led to a marked increase in demand for electrical power, and by the end of hostilities industrialists had realised this cleanly efficient power source could significantly increase productivity. The government was also aware that a domestic electrical supply could both transform Londoners' homes and abate the terrible smog that regularly enveloped the city. The problem was that the electricity supply was unsuited to domestic use.

At the time, London had no fewer than 13 electricity supply companies, all serving specific areas of the capital. These were set up to offer electricity in commercial volume, which remained far too expensive for most householders to consider. Before the war had taken precedence over everything else, the government had taken steps towards providing affordable domestic electricity by establishing an Electric Power Supply Committee. The committee had recommended that a series of electrical boards should be set up across the country, with responsibility for the generation and supply of power to each individual district. The war had prevented those plans from progressing any further, but in 1919 the Electricity

(Supply) Act brought them back to life. The new regional authorities would take control of all generators within their area and were also given authority to build new power stations where necessary. Consequently, the London board oversaw the construction of Battersea Power Station, which began in 1929 on the site of the old Southwark & Vauxhall Waterworks. As the supply of electricity became more regulated, so its usage gradually increased.

In 1926, the Central Electricity Board was created, which in turn established the National Grid – the network of power stations across the country. Industries were encouraged to use this new resource, which purported to be more reliable and cost-effective than private generators. In addition, the CEB worked with local councils to offer householders an affordable way to wire up their homes. Very slowly, the old gas mantles that had proliferated in homes across the UK gave way to electric light.

Under the streets, the huge clusters of electricity cables multiplied as the power source made its way into houses, offices, shops and factories. Streets that had once been dimly lit became bathed in electric light. London began to acquire a night-time glow visible from many miles away. By the mid-1930s, however, a new threat in Europe would plunge the glowing city back into darkness.

As the great power station at Battersea neared completion, Londoners watched apprehensively as the threat of a second war with Germany gradually increased. By 1938, the government began to prepare for what seemed to be an inevitable conflict. Realising that London would once again be a target for enemy bombing raids, they sought ways to protect the populace. London's subterranean labyrinth quickly took on a new role as a place of shelter for politicians, the armed forces and civilians alike. Government ministers even prepared to relocate Parliament outside the capital, though many politicians feared this move would appear as though leaders were deserting the public at their time of greatest need. Consequently, alternative premises were sought for the Prime Minister and his Cabinet beneath the capital's streets.

After much searching, it was decided that the basement of the Office of Works building at Storey's Gate was a suitable venue for the War Cabinet, being a five-minute walk from the Houses of Parliament. In June 1938, work began to convert this former storage area into a subterranean warren of offices and private rooms. The finished bunker (which became operational just one week before Germany's invasion of Poland) comprised a large committee room, a map room with the various theatres of war pasted on the walls, and a telephone room – a converted broom cupboard where enciphered telephone calls could be made. Later during the war, top-secret transatlantic telephone conversations were rendered unintelligible to the Germans through the Sigsaly scrambler. The London terminal for this hi-tech piece of equipment was so large that it could not be accommodated at Storey's Gate. Instead, it was installed in the basement of Selfridges Department Store, some distance away in Oxford Street.

The subterranean War Rooms also contained private living quarters for Winston Churchill and his aides, along with a small but fully functioning kitchen and a surprisingly suburban dining room. While the War Rooms were undeniably convenient, there were also fears that a sustained bombing raid on central London could render them inaccessible. The government therefore felt it prudent to find alternative underground accommodation in the suburbs.

Several secret locations were subsequently chosen, the most important of which was the Post Office Telecommunications Research Centre in the quiet north-west London backwater of Dollis Hill. This large but unremarkable building sat on an 8-acre strip of land sandwiched between sprawling Gladstone Park and the Welsh Harp reservoir. In the early 1930s, plans had been submitted to enlarge the complex, and the government, realising they could incorporate an underground HQ for the War Cabinet, now finally approved the scheme. Building work commenced and, as locals watched its innocuous progress, they little suspected that, beneath their feet, a huge basement was being excavated to play host to the country's most eminent politicians.

The underground citadel had virtually identical facilities to the Cabinet War Rooms at Storey's Gate, but its location 40ft below ground made it suitably impenetrable. The only rooms not incorporated into the complex were living quarters – a sprawling art deco apartment block called Neville's Court in nearby Dollis Hill Lane was requisitioned for this purpose.

This Emergency HQ was completed in June 1940, just three months before the onset of the Blitz. The War Cabinet issued it with the code name PADDOCK and ordered that it be made ready for immediate use. On 3 October, a trial meeting was held at the new underground HQ, but many were left distinctly unimpressed. Churchill himself stated that the accommodation was 'unsuited to the conditions which have arisen', but in truth he disliked the claustrophobic atmosphere and the lengthy trip from Westminster. In the eventuality, PADDOCK was only ever used by the War Cabinet on one further occasion – when visiting Australian Prime Minister Robert Menzies was taken there to debrief the Cabinet on his country's war effort. In the meantime, the search was on for more convenient premises closer to Westminster.

Churchill's replacement for PADDOCK was part of a curious development that occupied a plot of land bordered by Great Peter Street, Monck Street, Marsham Street and Horseferry Road in Westminster. The site had previously been occupied by two huge gas silos and a works building belonging to the Gas Light & Coke Company. The silos had been removed in 1937 and later, during the Blitz, a bomb fell on the disused site, destroying what remained of the works. Realising that it was ideally located, the government requisitioned the land and began redevelopment.

Two huge circular buildings were partly submerged in the holes left by the gas silos, newly christened the North and South Rotundas, with one sturdy steel-framed building replacing the old works. The Rotundas each comprised 3 storeys, only 1½ of which was visible at ground level. The North Rotunda was requisitioned for the new War Rooms and duly fitted out with a meeting room, map room, offices and telephone switchboard, as well as private living quarters. Deep below street level, a series of tunnels connected it with the War Office's headquarters at the Duke of Buccleuch's former residence at Montagu House, the Admiralty Office on Horseguards and several other important government buildings along Whitehall.

It transpired that PADDOCK was not the only wartime white elephant in the north-west London suburbs. Hidden under the government stationery offices on Headstone Lane, Harrow was the Air Ministry citadel, codenamed 'Station Z'. This underground fortress was completed in October 1940, deep below a new office block that, like the building at Dollis Hill, was primarily built to hide what lay beneath it. It contained a committee room, offices, a state-of-the-art telephone room housing a teletype machine (an early forerunner of email) and a switchboard linking the bunker directly to Whitehall. Those 'in the know' could get connected to this top-secret telephone system from anywhere in Britain by making a trunk call to Harrow 4269.

Not far away from the Air Ministry bunker was the Admiralty Citadel, codenamed 'IP'. This covert office complex was constructed underneath a new wing of the naval chart factory on Oxgate Lane, Cricklewood. Following the completion of both citadels, a skeleton staff known as 'the insurance party' was installed at both sites. Their task was to keep the offices functioning under total secrecy until their superiors arrived. As with PADDOCK, however, the two citadels were located too far away from Whitehall to be deemed useful. The insurance party remained until hostilities ceased, but afterwards the offices were closed down, never having played an active part in the war.

The purpose-built citadels proved unsuccessful mainly due to their relatively inaccessible suburban locations. However, in central London, finding sites that could be converted into secret war rooms without thousands of people realising it proved difficult. Ultimately, two locations close to the heart of the city would be utilised, both of which were in disused old Underground stations.

Down Street had once been a station on the Piccadilly & Brompton Railway (today's Piccadilly Line). When it opened in 1907, it was intended to serve the bustling district bordering Green Park, but proved unpopular due to twin factors: the lack of available space on Piccadilly itself resulted in the station entrance being hidden away down an unremarkable side road; it was also very close to two more prominent stations – Hyde Park Corner and Dover Street (now known as Green Park) – and located in one of London's wealthiest districts, where well-heeled residents preferred to use their own private transport rather than rely on the Tube.

Consequently, while nearby stations teemed with commuters, shoppers and sightseers, an empty Down Street languished. Just 11 years after it had opened, the Sunday service was cancelled; by 1932, the station was completely shut down. However, during the prelude to conflict in Europe, London's railway companies began to search for a bomb-proof operations room where they could keep trains running through the air raids. Down Street's central location and deep platforms (60ft below street level) provided a suitable, if potentially cramped, location.

Work began to convert the station into an emergency HQ in April 1939. Access to the subterranean site from street level was either via the original spiral staircase or a specially installed lift. Once below street level, the staff had to make their way through two heavy doors designed to protect against poison gas or deadly smoke from nearby fires. The doors opened onto a subway converted into a narrow room, where teams of typists sat along a narrow table facing the curved tunnel wall. Beyond the typing pool lay an office complex with a long committee room at its centre. Stairs at the end of the subway led down to the original platforms, now separated from the track by a brick wall. The platforms provided space for more offices, plus dormitories and even a kitchen. Toilet facilities, including baths, were located in the high-level subway that ran directly above the platforms.

The building work was unfinished when war broke out and the subterranean offices' first occupants were forced to work in rooms without doors or ceilings, where their papers and belongings were covered with layers of black dust and soot. However, by the beginning of 1940, the headquarters were completed and worked surprisingly well as an emergency command centre. Its central location also caught the attention of Churchill, who was constantly on the lookout for centrally located underground offices in which to convene emergency meetings, should the HQ at Storey's Gate be inaccessible. At his request, a disused air shaft was reconfigured to accommodate the War Cabinet. Although work on this new section was not completed until after the Blitz came to an end, Churchill did use the suite for safe sleeping quarters from the spring of 1941 until November 1943, when the North Rotunda was completed. Rumour has it that he would peruse the railway committee's minutes while prowling the corridors late at night, making anonymous notes and suggestions on the paperwork.

Like its counterparts in north-west London, the Down Street citadel was a carefully guarded secret. Its underground offices had no postal address (all letters were sent to an address in south-west London and forwarded by courier) and even the telephone number was redirected from Whitehall. Access to the HQ was gained through an anonymous doorway or via the Tube. Those 'in the know' rode in the driver's cab and were covertly dropped off at the bricked-up platforms near a small exit unnoticed by other travellers, who assumed the train had merely been held up in the tunnel. The platforms were also fitted with a special signal alerting the driver to stop, so that staff could exit the HQ under cover. Churchill's wife, Clementine, occasionally used this service to visit various air-raid shelters along the Underground railway network.

Further west along the Piccadilly & Brompton Railway line was Brompton Road station. Opened in 1906, it was never much used, as it was too far away from the Knightsbridge shops, and visitors to the nearby Victoria & Albert Museum generally preferred to disembark at South Kensington. By the time of World War 1, the booking office had closed due to lack of custom (tickets could be bought from vending machines or the lift attendants) and part of the ground floor had been converted into a club.

Despite the lack of passengers, the station remained open – although its few patrons were often frustrated by how many trains failed to stop there. This became a standing joke amongst commuters; in 1928, playwright Jevan Brandon-Thomas entitled his new comedy *Passing Brompton Road* – a phrase all too familiar to travellers on the line.

Brompton Road station struggled on into the 1930s, but, by 1934, improvement works and a new entrance for Knightsbridge station prompted its closure. Soon afterwards, its disused site caught the attention of the Victoria

& Albert Museum, then looking for a convenient place to protect its most valuable exhibits from air raids. However, although assurances were made to the museum that Brompton Road's underground tunnels would be made available, in the event the site was requisitioned by the First Anti-Aircraft Division, which constructed its HQ in the station's lift shaft.

The shaft was divided into five Gun Operations Rooms (or GORs), which sat directly on top of each other. The room located at the bottom of the lift shaft – GOR V – was the emergency room (which thankfully never had to be used). Above this was GOR IV, the operations centre for south London; above that, GOR III performed the same function for north London, while GOR II housed a telephone exchange whereby intelligence was relayed to the officers stationed there.

The uppermost room – GOR I – was the domain of the General Officer Commanding. In this airless shaft, the progress of air raids on London was charted by women from the Auxiliary Territorial Service (ATS), who moved markers around tabletop grids to simulate what was happening in the skies above the city. On a raised dais above them sat the commanding officers, who interpreted the information before issuing commands to their RAF colleagues, the fire services and the Air Raid Patrols. On the walls surrounding the tables, maps showing the location of anti-aircraft stations lit up when the guns were firing.

The atmosphere in the Brompton Road lift shaft during a bombing raid was intense. The complex system of tracking enemy aircraft while simultaneously directing a response demanded a huge amount of concentration, as any lapses could potentially lead to loss of life. Staff at this strange headquarters therefore needed somewhere to unwind and the Gladstone Pub, located next to the station entrance, became a popular and convenient watering hole, humorously referred to as GOR VI.

In addition to providing secure refuges for ministers and their staff, the government was also faced with the problem of how to protect the public during an air raid. While everyone agreed that the most sensible and cost-effective course of action was for people to take shelter at home, they realised that thousands of people would be miles away from their houses when the Luftwaffe struck. Consequently, the construction of public shelters was discussed at length in the weeks and months that prefigured the Blitz.

Psychologists warned that crowds forced into subterranean bunkers for hours on end could develop a 'shelter mentality', forming troglodyte communities with a distrust of outsiders. Acting on this advice, the government initially decided to build a series of shallow 'trench shelters' just a few feet below ground. These public citadels took the form of concrete-lined underground compartments set at angles to each other, to limit damage if a bomb landed nearby. They were accessed by a series of ramps that led to long, low rooms flanked with wooden benches, with recesses containing extremely basic toilet facilities in the corner of each. Square openings in the ceilings, protected by heavy iron shutters, gave an alternative route out of the bunker if the ramps should become blocked by debris.

Every district of London was encouraged to build trench shelters in any public space large enough to accommodate them. For instance, in Westminster, Hyde Park, Green Park and St James's Park all acquired shelters, along with Eaton, Vincent, St George's and Golden Squares, accommodating an estimated 14,000 people.

In addition to purpose-built trench shelters, other subterranean spaces were converted into makeshift bunkers. The old arches under the Adelphi Buildings, on the bank of the Thames, provided accommodation for up to 600 people; church crypts were opened to the public; even coalholes connected to small shops were reinforced with concrete and fitted with escape hatches knocked into party walls.

The larger department stores also made arrangements to protect shoppers in the event of an air raid. Harrods built a concrete and steel fortress in the centre of their shop for customers, with staff instructed to shelter in the basement of the store – handily already linked to the warehouse across Brompton Road via the series of tunnels constructed just before World War 1 by Harley Dalrymple-Hay. Selfridges proudly announced there was space for several thousand people in their basement (yet to be filled by the Sigsaly scrambler). In Regent Street, Dickins & Jones constructed a special air-raid shelter for use during business hours and also converted their basement into a 24-hour public shelter.

Across the Thames, in Southwark, the limited amount of suitable space for trench shelters led to the construction of a colossal deep-level shelter, 70ft beneath Borough High Street and capable of accommodating up to 14,000 people on its own.

At first it seemed that the frenzied construction of the shelters, which caused a considerable amount of mess and disruption, may have been unwarranted. In the first few months after Britain entered the war, the threatened bombardment from the skies failed to materialise. Underground bunkers stood empty across the capital. However, on 7 September 1940, Hitler unleashed a terrifying air campaign in an attempt to bring the British government to its knees.

Late in the afternoon, nearly 350 German bombers and over 600 fighter planes appeared in the autumn sky over London, beginning a relentless two-hour bombardment of the city. Later that evening, another wave of enemy aircraft continued the campaign of destruction. The aerial assault continued until 4.30am the following morning. The Blitz had started, and for the next 57 days London was rocked by repeated bombing raids.

The previously redundant air-raid shelters suddenly filled with shocked and anxious Londoners. Many had experienced air raids during World War 1, but nothing had prepared them for this onslaught. Nevertheless, the indomitable British war spirit prevailed. The soulless concrete shelters became sanctuaries where an apprehensive population found strength in companionship. It quickly became apparent that most Londoners preferred to take cover in the larger shelters, where they felt less isolated.

As the bombs rained down on London, the government became increasingly concerned about conditions in public shelters. These bleak, oppressive rooms had been designed to accommodate people for only a couple of hours, but some of the larger shelters had become all-night dormitories. Fearing these enclosed spaces were potential breeding grounds for contagious disease, the government dispatched royal physician Lord Horder to report back on what he found. After visiting several public shelters across the city, Horder concluded that while those in central London were undeniably overcrowded, they were at least well organised and clean. The real danger lay in the suburban shelters, which were not so stringently regulated by the wardens. The biggest problem was that the largely unsupervised incumbents often left their bedding down in the shelter, where it festered amid the heavy atmosphere, propagating germs. Steps were taken to improve supervision in these shelters, but the chaos that ensued during a bombing raid made enforcement of regulations virtually impossible.

Although public shelters were undeniably inhospitable, the press and government did their best to present them in a positive light. The Minister for Home Security, John Anderson, was fond of disseminating amusing stories of life in the shelters, one of which involved a young mother who took her child down during an air raid. In order to distract the boy from the tense atmosphere, she began to sing to him, at which point the child looked at her and said, 'Do you think you can stop singing, Mother? I want to hear the bombs go off.'

Animal exploits were popular fodder for journalists in search of a cheery story. Although they were not supposed to be given access, a surprisingly diverse menagerie found its way into London's public shelters – including Billy, a tame badger found hiding in a Regent's Park bunker, a great crested grebe which sought sanctuary at Euston, and a stray cat which regularly joined the queue for a public shelter at Brixton.

For most shelter dwellers, camaraderie did not detract from the terrifying reality of what was happening above ground. Elderly people died from sheer shock and the child who wanted to hear the bombs dropping was unusual (if not apocryphal). Herbert Manton, who lived at Agate Street, Canning Town and was 12 years old when the Blitz began, described for this writer sitting in a public shelter during an intense daytime raid, wondering what he would find once the all-clear siren sounded. 'It was not knowing what was happening that was the worst part,' he remembered. 'You could hear the bombs going off close by, but you didn't know what had been hit.' Herbert also recalled the atmosphere in the shelter as the bombing grew louder. 'We knew the bombs were getting closer and we all sort of froze. I looked across at my aunt who was sitting opposite me and what I saw in her eyes was pure terror.' Herbert and his family eventually emerged from the shelter to find that their house had been completely destroyed.

One of the greatest fears harboured by occupants of the shelters was being buried by a bomb blast. Unfortunately, this fear was not unfounded. On 21 September 1940, *The Times* reported: 'A bomb which fell in a park in North London [the previous night] struck one of the emergency escape shafts of an underground shelter. Some of the occupants were injured by the blast; others were buried alive under tons of earth.'

Four days later, a bomb fell on an underground shelter serving a block of council flats in east London. Several people were killed by the blast, including newlyweds Charles and Rose Mariner. The *Daily Mirror* reported: 'The bomb struck the side wall of the shelter after ploughing through the ground. The Mariners were found lying in the corner of the wall which took the full blast. Their bodies were covered with about a ton of earth and concrete. One of the rescue workers said, "Their arms were clasped tightly round each other and their lips were touching. It is obvious that the husband had flung himself across his wife to try to protect her."'

When the days began to grow colder, life in the shelters became even more unpleasant as they had no form of heating. As the bombs continued to fall on the capital, myriad ways were sought in which to make the daily visits more tolerable. Mr H. Rottenburg of King's College, Cambridge wrote to *The Times*, suggesting the bunkers could be fitted with Roman-style under-floor heating, while the King was dispatched to the shelters to boost public morale. After hearing horror stories from the inhabitants of an East End shelter, he displayed how touched he was by the plight of his people, telling them, 'I think you are all so wonderful in the way you are carrying on in spite of it all.'

Although Londoners were demonstrating remarkable fortitude, the fact remained that their city was being systematically destroyed. As more and more homes were devastated and domestic basements and garden shelters rendered useless, an ever growing crowd of people sought sanctuary at the public shelters. Realising that the situation had to be improved before winter set in, the new Minister for Home Security, Herbert Morrison, planned to build more deep-level shelters. In order to alleviate queues outside the existing shelters, he also introduced a ticket system whereby space would be allotted according to need. Mothers and their children would be issued with priority tickets. Once this group had been catered for, the remaining allocation would be distributed among those living or working closest to the shelter. In addition to this, Morrison decided to ignore previous reservations and open up the Tube stations as refuges.

Although the Underground railway had been used for shelter during World War 1 with little incident, it was felt that the sheer number of people on the platforms would warrant the enforcement of special rules and regulations. Posters therefore appeared on all station platforms, stating:

> *In order to prevent the movement of passengers being obstructed, two white lines are being painted on each platform, one 4ft from the edge of the platform and the other 8ft from the edge of the platform.*

> *Nobody will be allowed to shelter in the stations before 4pm or reserve places at any time.*

> *Between 4pm and 7.30pm sheltering will be allowed between the platform wall and the white line farthest from the platform edge and after 7.30pm, between the wall and the line nearest the edge of the platform.*

> *Nobody will be allowed to shelter in any passageway before 7.30pm except in large circulating areas, where a portion will be marked off for this purpose.*

The Tube shelters were popular as soon as they opened, not least because they were considerably warmer and more hospitable than the purpose-built shelters. As the weather worsened, the platforms became crowded with people, and some enterprising youngsters found that good money was to be made by reserving places, for which they could charge up to a shilling every night. Sidney Scurridge, aged 13, from East Acton, told a reporter from the *Daily Mirror*, 'I have stood for hours outside Tube stations. Sometimes I miss school. Policemen have advised me to take shelter during air raids [but] when I have done so, I have found my place taken in the queue.'

As the demand for shelter increased and Londoners were forced to pay nightly visits to the underground sanctuaries, the government discussed ways to make the air-raid shelters more hospitable. The catering trade and voluntary bodies such as the Salvation Army were encouraged to make nightly visits to the public shelters to distribute a warming, comforting selection of foods such as soup, pies and cake, along with tea and coffee, all at reasonable prices.

Catering in the Tube stations was handled by London Transport, which set up regular food services in numerous central London stations by November 1940. Every evening, a team of women 'clad in green frocks, with bright red kerchiefs on their heads' walked down the platforms laden with provisions. *The Times* described the scene:

'Some carry giant teapots from which they serve tea at 1d a cup (or you may have cocoa at the same price). Others carry a tray of refreshments – buns and pieces of cake, 1d; apples 1½d; meat pies, 1½d; bars of chocolate, 2d; and packets of biscuits, 2d.'

Each station was fitted with electrically heated boilers to make the endless pots of tea and coffee and to heat babies' bottles. The provisions were delivered during the afternoon via special trains.

In addition to the mobile canteens, many public air-raid shelters were kitted out with libraries, games rooms and radios so that the inhabitants could keep in touch with the outside world. Some even offered evening classes. In one Westminster shelter, local artist Edgar Willings commandeered a room and turned it into a makeshift studio where he and his fellow refugees could draw and paint. Surprisingly, Mr Willings saw beauty in the cramped conditions. 'There are terrific possibilities here for an artist,' he asserted. 'Time and again I have been struck by the grouping and lovely patches of colour.' Most shelters were not fortunate enough to have the services of men like Willings at their disposal, and their nightly ritual was rather more mundane. In January 1941, a reader wrote to the *Daily Mirror* describing a typical evening in their public shelter:

5.50pm – Enter shelter. Listen to 6 o'clock news. Loud speakers are placed in convenient spots.

6.30-7.30pm – Read or write in a room provided.

7.30-9.00pm – Game of cards in the card room.

9.30pm – Light suppers are brought round.

10.30pm – Make up bunk and go to sleep.

Our shelter is air-conditioned, centrally heated, electrically lit. Services are held every Sunday and we have occasional talkies [film shows].

As winter set in, the nightly descent into the underground shelters became decidedly unpleasant. The air raids showed no sign of abating and the public bunkers grew more inhospitable as cold and wet weather set in. By November 1940, the smaller, hastily built shelters across London were beginning to leak. Water settled in the concrete-lined compartments, sometimes inches deep. With no drainage, it had to be swept or pumped out by the wardens. In some shelters, conditions became so bad that inmates had to build themselves platforms out of orange boxes to avoid sitting with their feet submerged in muddy water.

Even the Tube shelters were not as impregnable as Londoners had hoped. During a raid on 14 October 1940 a huge bomb fell outside Balham Tube station, creating a massive crater in the roadway. In the immediate aftermath of the blast, a bus driver lost control of his vehicle and ploughed into the massive hole, causing yet more damage. The water main and sewers running beneath the road ruptured, spewing muddy water into the crater at a frightening rate. Underneath the blast, the badly damaged roof of the northbound Tube platform collapsed and escaping water gushed onto the approximately 600 people sheltering there. The occupants desperately tried to get out of the tunnel as it filled with water and debris, but the exits were too narrow for a speedy evacuation. Sixty-six men, women and children never managed to escape the tunnel, drowning in the filthy water.

By the end of November 1940, many shelters bore little resemblance to the cosy retreats described in the newspapers. Local resident Margaret Corbett-Ashby wrote a damning description of those in the East End: 'There are shelters in East London where, by the sole illumination of a hurricane lantern, the visitor picks his steps among human bodies huddled on the mud floors, fearful of treading on a human face, and where the wetness of the walls is easier to feel than see ... Improvements are visible, especially in the largest and most publicised shelters, which hold thousands and attract official notice, while those which hold hundreds remain neglected. Will improvement come and by whom will it be made?'

In response to the outcry concerning the poor conditions of some shelters, the government issued a limp directive advising inmates on how to look after themselves. Among the sage advice contained in 'Health Hints for Shelter Nights' were instructions to gargle with salt in order to prevent the spread of cold viruses, not to spit, to keep feet dry by wearing extra socks and to provide extra warmth by heating bricks in the oven and wrapping them in towels.

Little was done to improve the smaller shelters as discussions were underway to build a new series of deep-level public citadels across central London. This type of refuge had been discussed back in the late 1930s, but at the time it had been rejected as too expensive and liable to cause the dreaded 'bunker mentality'. However, contrary to psychologists' doom-laden warnings, Londoners had displayed no tendency to stay underground any longer than absolutely necessary. The unparalleled destruction caused thus far by the Blitz also prompted the government to make a U-turn. On 3 November 1940, Herbert Morrison announced that deep-shelter accommodation in the Tube network was to be extended by boring a new series of tunnels.

The new shelters would each comprise two tunnels measuring 16½ft in diameter by 12,000ft long. Each would be divided horizontally into two floors incorporating bunks, cooking facilities, bathrooms and medical bays. It was initially proposed that a total of 10 deep-level shelters would be built, with five to be located under the south London Tube stations at Clapham South, Clapham Common, Clapham North, Stockwell and the Oval, and then again across the river at Goodge Street, Camden Town, Belsize Park, Chancery Lane and St Paul's. In order to recoup some of the considerable cost, it was intended that, after the war, the tunnels would be linked together to create a high-speed underground rail network across the city.

Work on the new shelters began on 27 November 1940, amidst blistering Luftwaffe attacks designed to beat London into submission. As men and women worked tirelessly to keep the city running under truly appalling conditions, there was an eventual shortage of labourers to work at the construction sites.

In addition, materials grew scarce as the docks faced almost daily disruption, or indeed devastation, by the enemy bombers. Initially, the government had hoped to have the shelters ready by the summer of 1941, but, as time went on, this deadline seemed increasingly unlikely to be met. By the spring of that year, the relentless enemy raids caused many Londoners to wonder how much longer their city could survive. As work on the new shelters made its painfully slow progress, however, the air raids suddenly stopped. The last raid of the London Blitz occurred on 10 May 1941, when an attack on Westminster left 1,300 civilians dead and over 1,600 injured. Following that, the skies fell silent.

As it gradually became apparent that the incessant bombing raids had come to an end (at least for the time being), many civilians began to regard the new deep-level shelters as a wanton waste of money. However, fearing another wave of attacks, the government was loath to abandon the project. The works at St Paul's and the Oval (both of which were proving unexpectedly challenging) were abandoned, but construction of the remaining shelters continued. By the time they were completed in the winter of 1942, however, fears of a new Blitz had subsided and the government decided to put them to alternative use. The majority of the shelters were used to billet British troops, while the Goodge Street site was made available to General Eisenhower for a US command centre.

Although further sustained bombing raids on London had not materialised, repeated attacks on the rest of Britain kept the capital on alert – particularly following Allied raids on Berlin, on 1 March 1943. On reading about the raid the next day, many Londoners thought it prudent to spend the next few nights in the deep-level shelters. On 2 March in Bethnal Green, where the unfinished Central Line Tube station provided shelter for up to 10,000 people, local residents spent an uneventful night. By the next evening, many were considering staying at home when the air-raid warning began to sound. As the sirens wailed, hundreds of families wearily packed up their bedding and made their way to the Tube shelter, where a crowd had already gathered at the top of the steps. They began to make their way down to the platforms, but, as they were doing so, a new type of anti-aircraft missile screamed through the night sky. Scared by the unfamiliar noise, the crowd began to push its way into the station. Close to the bottom of the stairs, a young woman lost her footing and tumbled down the remaining steps, causing those behind her to fall forward. Unaware of what was happening at the bottom of the stairwell, the anxious crowd at the top kept pushing forward. People who fell were unable to get up, as the crowd surged down the steps and entrances to the platform tunnels became blocked by bodies. By the time those at the top of the stairs realised what was happening, it was too late: 173 people lost their lives in London's worst civilian disaster of the war.

Despite the tragedy at Bethnal Green, the purpose-built deep-level shelters remained closed to the public until Germany launched its V-Weapons offensive in June 1944. The deep-level refuges were finally opened up to Londoners, with three exceptions: Goodge Street continued to be occupied by US troops; Clapham Common was retained for government use; Chancery Lane was by now the emergency command HQ for several government bodies, including the Port of London Authority, the London Civil Defence Department and the mysterious Inter Services Research Bureau – a branch of MI6 created to assist resistance operations in countries under German occupation.

The new public shelters proved singularly unpopular with Londoners, mainly because they were so far underground. Refugees had to descend 130ft into the bowels of the city, where they felt dangerously cut off from the world. Old fears of being buried alive re-emerged, as the public surmised that while a trench shelter could be easily accessed by rescue workers, it might take weeks for aid to reach the deep-level refuges.

Ultimately, most of the deep-level shelters were a waste of money and resources. They remained over half-empty during the subsequent raids and were finally decommissioned in May 1945. In the financially stretched aftermath of World War 2, the high-speed rail link would be forgotten and the tunnels lay abandoned under the city streets.

Over the following decade, shattered London would begin to rebuild itself. Churchill had likened the city to 'some huge prehistoric animal, capable of enduring terrible injuries, mangled and bleeding from many wounds and yet preserving its life and movement', but it was ordinary Londoners who regenerated the metropolis, achieving this monumental task in the face of adversity.

The people who rebuilt the city after the war did so in mourning. In addition to the thousands of soldiers who fell defending their country, over 53,000 British civilians were killed by enemy action between 1940 and 1945, with many more sustaining life-changing injuries. A large proportion of these men, women and children had lived in London.

CHAPTER 7

THE UNDERGROUND UNDERWORLD

The chaos and destruction of the bombing raids on London during World War 2 provided ample opportunities for the city's criminal element. Once the war was over, some young men found it difficult to adjust to a normal civilian life and became part of an underworld network that would continue to cause a great deal of trouble for the police.

One such gang went on the rampage in the autumn of 1955, beginning their crime spree in an Underground railway station. In the early hours of 1 October, booking clerk Horace Searle was alone in the ticket office at Highbury when a man burst through the door, announcing in threatening tones, 'This is a stick-up. Don't move or touch that telephone, or I'll shoot.' Searle quickly realised that the man was deadly serious and, with a gun pointed at his head, tremulously opened the office safe. By this time, the gunman had been joined by a second man wielding a large hammer. The terrified booking clerk nervously stood back and watched helplessly as the men grabbed the meagre £5 that lay inside the safe.

Quite why the two men risked so much for a miserable £5 remained a mystery, but the robbery did nothing to slake their thirst for ill-gotten gains. The police later caught up with the thieves as they swerved through the narrow streets of Mayfair after robbing a jeweller's store. The two men leaned out of the windows, peppering the squad car with a hail of bullets as they sped through London's most upmarket district. John Cohen, a 25-year-old labourer from Harlesden, and his accomplices – Ronald Parsons, 22 and John Cotten, 29 – were apprehended a few days later. Cohen was sentenced to 20 years in prison. Parsons received a 12-year sentence and Cotten was sent down for 10 years.

John Cohen's fruitless raid on Highbury Underground station continued a long tradition of crime committed beneath the streets of London. The subterranean spaces under the city had long since been a popular resort for criminals.

During the 18th century, the stinking open sewers that ran through the metropolis provided a handy, if unpleasant, escape route for felons on the run. On the evening of 5 August 1772, William Kitchen, a marble polisher from Marylebone, was taking a stroll with his lady friend Elizabeth Spencer down a rural lane that ran from the outskirts of the West End to the turnpike at Tottenham Court Road. This remote but well-used track was well known in the area as a haunt of highwaymen and footpads, who lurked behind trees or hedges to relieve the unsuspecting of their valuables. That night, William and Elizabeth made their way along the quiet lane, unaware that they were being stalked by notorious thieves George Kem and Benjamin Johnson.

As the couple reached a particularly deserted spot, Kem and Johnson saw their chance and leapt out into the roadway, brandishing pistols. William Kitchen later recalled how Johnson 'bid me stand, or he said he would blow my brains out [and] bid me deliver my money; he repeated that several times over. I delivered him first a shilling and then another.'

Not content with a couple of shillings, Johnson forced Kitchen to hand over his silver pocket-watch while his accomplice took a silver thimble from Elizabeth – the only item she carried of any worth. Finally satisfied that the terrified couple had nothing more worth stealing, the two footpads sent them on their way, threatening that if they dared turn around they would shoot them.

William and Elizabeth stumbled down the lane, dazed from their ordeal. Luckily, they had not gone far before they spotted two night-watchmen who took off in the direction of the footpads, taking Kitchen with them to identify the thieves. They soon caught sight of the two felons making their way across a moonlit field, near a coaching inn known as Farthing Pye House. By the time they reached the inn, the two men had disappeared but the patrons told them they had seen Benjamin Johnson disappearing into the common sewer that ran outside.

The sewer was typical of the dilapidated old ditches that coursed through London at the end of the 18th century, around 4ft deep and partially covered by an archway. A witness at the subsequent court hearing explained that its sides had long since been broken down by the dung carts that deposited their foul contents. The search party made their way to the opening closest to where the men were last spotted, extending a candle under the dark arch. It was there, slumped in the fetid slurry, that they found Johnson. The slow-witted thief had partaken of a little too much Dutch courage before the robbery and was now almost insensible. William Kitchen's property was found half-buried in the sewer wall, a few inches away from Johnson's discarded pistol.

With Johnson now under arrest, the constables went on searching for Kem, who was eventually apprehended in Spur Street, near Leicester Fields (today's Leicester Square). Once in custody, the two prisoners fervently protested their innocence. Ultimately hauled in front of a judge at the Old Bailey, despite the appearance of several witnesses who vouched for their good character, the men were sentenced to death.

Although the open sewers were rapidly buried beneath the streets of the expanding city in the 19th century, some were still used as criminal lairs as late as the 1830s. In 1835, 19-year-old George Newman sought sanctuary in a Westminster sewer whilst attempting to escape from a robbery at the counting house of Richard Brooks, a tallow chandler whose premises were on Southwark Bridge Road.

On 14 March, Newman and three accomplices broke through the roof of Mr Brooks' property and made off with his petty cash box, containing half a crown, four shillings and 15 pennies. On making their escape they were discovered, splitting up in a bid to lose their pursuers. Newman made for the open sewer behind the premises, thinking it an ideal place to hide until the search party gave up. However, he was being watched by William Taylor, a 12-year-old schoolboy who lived in the house opposite Mr Brooks.

At the subsequent trial, the boy stated: 'I was in Little Guildford Street, at the back of Mr Brooks' premises … I saw [Newman] before he got into the ditch – he came off Mr Brooks' premises, onto [an adjoining] wall, got on the privy, then jumped down and got into the ditch. I heard the policeman's rattle and told him where Newman was gone. They went there and found him.'

PC William Clark Hunt continued: 'I took Newman out of the ditch – it is the common sewer – he was up to his knees in it under the arch. I took him to the station house, searched him and found a Lucifer-box and some matches in his pocket. I went back and examined the premises. I went out of the trap door on the roof and found the petty cash box there broken open.'

Despite the fact that they were all still in their teens, Newman and his partners in crime paid heavily for stealing Mr Brooks' petty cash box. They were sentenced to death for taking money that did not even amount to £1.

London's sewers were not the only subterranean hiding places favoured by 19th-century criminals. In the 1840s, entrepreneur Samuel Bentall hit on the lucrative idea of setting up a market in the meandering depths of the Thames Tunnel, letting pitches to local traders. The underground market was a great success, attracting a good deal of custom, but, unfortunately for Mr Bentall and

THE "SILENT HIGHWAY"-MAN.
"Your MONEY or your LIFE!"

ABOVE: *Punch* cartoon commenting on the putrid state of the Thames, 1858.
Mary Evans Picture Library

BELOW: The Fleet River near St Pancras, 1825. *Old and New London*

ABOVE LEFT: Charles
Pearson, *circa* 1855. *London
Transport Museum*

ABOVE RIGHT: Cartoon
depicting Joseph Bazalgette,
Punch 1883. *Mary Evans
Picture Library*

LEFT: Section showing the
various levels of Brunel's
Thames Tunnel. © *Junko
Yanigasawa, dRMM Architects*

ABOVE: The Crystal Palace subway. © *Mark Blundell Photography*

BELOW: Section showing the proposed Baker Street Station, 1860. *London Transport Museum*

ABOVE: A train of 'Long Charley' coaches hauled by a Gooch 2-4-0 steam locomotive at Praed Street Junction, Paddington, *circa* 1864. *London Transport Museum*

BELOW: The first underground train journey on the Metropolitan Railway at Edgware Road, 24 May 1864. *London Transport Museum*

ABOVE: Labourers working inside the frame of a Greathead Shield during the construction of the Central London Railway, 1897. *London Transport Museum*

BELOW: British Museum station, shortly after it opened. *London Transport Museum*

LEFT: The Blackwall Tunnel under construction.
Courtesy of Newham Heritage and Archives

BELOW: The Post Office Railway switch cabin,
1935. © *Royal Mail Group Ltd 2012, courtesy
of the British Postal Museum & Archive*

ABOVE: Brompton Road underground station, 1907. *London Transport Museum*

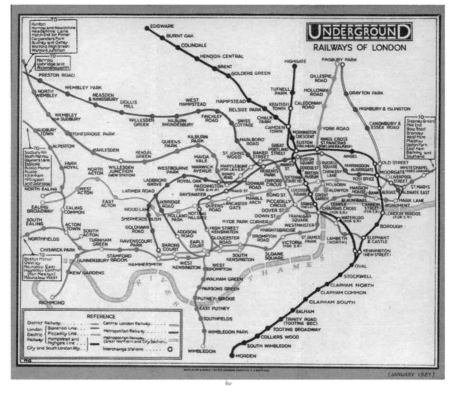

ABOVE: Tube map, 1927. *London Transport Museum*

BELOW: The booking hall of York Road station, 1927. *London Transport Museum*

LEFT: Factory workers descending into an air-raid shelter at Acton, 1940. *London Transport Museum*

LEFT: Subterranean air-raid shelter at Bethnal Green, *circa* 1940. *London Transport Museum*

BELOW: Escalators at Canary Wharf station. © *Janet Hall/RIBA Library Photographs Collection*

his stallholders, it also caught the attention of criminals. Thefts were common, as it was very difficult for busy traders to keep an eye on their stock and serve customers simultaneously. By 1845, the situation had got so bad that Amelia Elliott, who ran a stall selling household trinkets, decided to tackle the problem.

Ms Elliott's determination to end crime in the tunnel market resulted in her viewing any visitor to the stall with the utmost suspicion. Inevitably, her paranoia was sometimes misplaced. On 1 March 1845, she had customer Ann Kipping arrested for stealing a pin cushion, a scent box and three chimney ornaments from her stall. According to the zealous Ms Elliott, Kipping had asked her to look under the stall for a pot stand and then, while her back was turned, snatched the items and hid them under her cloak. The prisoner protested that she had never done anything of the sort, having picked up a decorative jar while Elliott was looking for the pot stand and paying for it before leaving the stall. The court found in the prisoner's favour. Ann Kipping was released but, despite the embarrassing mistake, her accuser was undeterred.

Amelia Elliott's crusade met with greater success later that year, when Mary Ann Williams, aged 20, tried to dispose of counterfeit coins at the market stall. Williams had purchased a 'trifling article' with a coin of high denomination, for which she received a large amount of change. A few minutes later, she returned to the stall and accused Ms Elliott of passing a forged half-sovereign. Incensed, Elliott told the woman she did not have any counterfeit coins and that Williams must have swapped it when she left the stand. Realising her trick had been found out, Mary Ann Williams quickly passed the coin to her companion, Daniel Garrard, who put it in his mouth and swallowed it, rather stupidly underlining their guilt.

Williams and Garrard were duly arrested and sent to trial at the Old Bailey, charged with dealing in counterfeit coins. Realising that Garrard's foolhardy action meant that Mary Ann Williams would almost certainly be found guilty, her lawyer tried to argue that the crime should not be tried as it took place under the bed of the Thames, beyond the jurisdiction of all courts. Unfortunately, the judge did not agree and Mary Ann Williams was sentenced to nine months' imprisonment with hard labour. The hapless Garrard was acquitted.

In addition to Mr Bentall's regular market, the Thames Tunnel was also the venue for occasional fairs. These below-ground events were extremely popular with the public. In March 1850, the Thames Tunnel Company staged a Grand Fancy Fair to celebrate the anniversary of its opening, as a *Times* journalist reported: 'The entire length of the tunnel and either shaft were decorated with myriads of variegated lamps, the panels being filled in with a variety of paintings, representing the most interesting views along the banks [of the Thames]. Rows of stalls, covered with ornamental articles, shows, refreshment booths, the Wizard of the North [Scottish magician John Anderson], Ethiopian Minstrels and bands of music were the amusements offered. During the day several thousand persons visited the tunnel.'

The huge attendance at these extravaganzas provided rich pickings for thieves, as John Francis discovered when he visited in March 1856. Mr Francis, a sailor from Well Street near the London Docks, was walking through the tunnel one evening when he felt someone pulling at his pocket-watch. He put his hand up to his waistcoat pocket, caught hold of the thief's hand and held it fast. The thief managed to pass the watch on to an accomplice, however, who quickly melted into the crowd.

From 1829, felons arrested in the sewers and foot tunnels that ran under the city were dealt with by the Metropolitan Police. However, elsewhere in London's subterranean labyrinth, the railway companies employed their own staff to maintain law and order beneath the streets.

The first railway police force was established in the 1830s on the overground Liverpool & Manchester Railway, with several other lines quickly following suit. Each force was a completely separate entity but all were modelled on the regular police. In London, railway police officers earned comparable wages to their counterparts in the Metropolitan Police and were organised into a similar hierarchy. They were distinguishable by the colour of their uniforms (for example, officers employed by the Great Western Railway wore scarlet tunics in contrast to the Met's blue) and their truncheons were painted with the crest of the railway company for whom they worked.

The early transport police were employed to ensure safety rather than prevent or detect crime. Each officer was issued with flags, a lamp and a watch, and was responsible for overseeing the safe arrival and departure of trains. When mechanical signalling was introduced, officers found themselves with more time for crime prevention but were still regularly sidetracked by general railway duties, such as changing points and supervising the loading of freight onto trains. Consequently, for the remainder of the 19th century, the transport police remained a disparate collection of forces which, while skilled in the smooth running of railways, had little experience of catching criminals.

This lack of experience is underlined by the first recorded arrest on the underground railway, the apprehension of John Reid in 1867 for the heinous crime of pulling a porter's beard. Reid had committed the offence after he and his friends were reprimanded by the porter at Gower Street station for displaying their dislike of the smoky atmosphere by 'coughing outrageously'. He was fined £3 for his insolence but nothing was done to remedy the choking atmosphere in Gower Street, or indeed any other station. Smoky railway carriages would continue to be a point of controversy until smoking was finally banned, over 100 years later.

During the early years of the underground railway, most troublesome smoke emanated from the engine itself. Despite engineers' attempts at retaining it in a boiler while the train was in a tunnel, a certain amount would escape and billow its way into the carriages. This unpleasant atmosphere was compounded by fumes from pipes and cigars and so, by 1870, the Metropolitan Railway took the decision to ban smoking in carriages whilst underground.

This caused a good deal of confusion among passengers, who failed to see why they could smoke in the train while it was above ground but had to stop once it tunnelled beneath the metropolis. In 1871, Albert Macklin of the Admiralty Registry Office was issued with a court summons charging him with smoking in a Metropolitan Railway carriage. At the trial, prosecuting barrister Montagu Williams declared that a letter had been sent to the directors of the Board of Trade, highlighting the enormous number of complaints about smoking in underground railway carriages. He also criticised the Metropolitan Railway Company's lackadaisical attitude, recommending they should be forced to provide separate smoking carriages if they declined to prosecute those who persisted.

In defence of the smokers, Mr Macklin highlighted the rather farcical system that then prevailed. He described a journey in a smoking carriage on the Great Western Railway's Windsor line when, upon arrival at Bishops Road station, he was told smoking was not allowed. Macklin showed the guard his ticket from Windsor and drew his attention to the fact that overground railways were required to provide smoking carriages in all their trains. The guard replied that this did not apply once the trains had reached Bishops Road, telling him that 'smoking carriage' signs were always removed at this point.

In response, Macklin argued that smoking carriages were attached to Great Northern and Midland trains on the underground railway. He also pointed out that to remove the sign from a smoking carriage, and then force non-smokers to board a compartment in which several men had been smoking, caused much greater inconvenience to the public than the maintenance of separate carriages.

Despite the validity of the defendant's argument, the judge upheld that the

Metropolitan Railway's bylaws should be observed by any train running on their lines. He fined Mr Macklin 10 shillings plus a further 10 shillings in costs.

∞

More serious crimes perpetrated on the Victorian Tube system were largely dealt with by the Metropolitan or City Police. They were kept busy even before the first underground railway was completed.

One evening in May 1862, labourers Edward Gregory and James Driscoll where working high above the line at King's Cross, fixing the metal girders that would form the roof of the new underground station. While the two men were precariously balanced on one of the iron rafters, a petty argument suddenly turned violent. Gregory lost his temper and began to violently punch Driscoll in the face and chest. In self defence, Driscoll picked up a spanner and walloped Gregory to make him stop. Enraged, Gregory pushed his workmate and sent him plunging 50ft from the top of the girder.

Labourers working at the bottom of the cutting rushed over to find Driscoll in a terrible state. He was rushed to the Royal Free Hospital, where the following day surgeon John D. Hill issued a grim statement: 'I hereby certify that James Driscoll was brought to the hospital last evening at seven o'clock suffering from severe compound fracture of both legs with severe shock to the system. Amputation of one leg was performed … and it is feared that the same operation will be imperative on the other limb. He is at the present time in a very precarious state and quite unable to make any statement.'

Driscoll quickly succumbed to his dreadful injuries. His appalled employer, the contractor John Jay, offered to pay for his funeral and his colleagues organised a collection for his widow, who would be left distraught and destitute by his death. His attacker was only saved from a murder trial by his workmates, however, who testified that Driscoll had slipped and fallen off the girder in the heat of the altercation. Gregory was found guilty of manslaughter and sentenced to 12 months' hard labour.

As soon as the underground railway opened, the police faced new challenges. The crowds on the new Metropolitan Line provided perfect prey for thieves and pickpockets. Passing themselves off as passengers, gangs of scoundrels roamed the busy platforms. Pocket-watches were particularly popular swag, as they were easily detached from the owner's waistcoat and could be disposed of quickly via one of London's numerous fences.

In January 1877, a clergyman was relieved of his pocket-watch while trying to board an underground train at Westminster Bridge Station. As he told *The Times*: 'I was with a party of seven, of whom four were children and there was a great crowd. I reached the platform with my tickets and at once found myself swayed about by the throng around me. I was thrown off my guard by my desire to keep close to my young people and to find seats for them.'

As a train pulled into the station, the crowd grew ever more dense as people stood back to allow passengers off the carriages, while others pushed to the front of the queue to secure a seat. The vicar's 12-year-old son was separated from him and, as he battled through the crush to get to the boy, he felt a tug on his watch chain. He spun round in time to see a well-dressed young man beating a hasty retreat from the platform, flitting through the crowd in the direction of the station exit.

The clergyman assumed the man had made off with his watch and tried to pursue him. By the time the vicar had forced his way through the bustling throng, however, the object of his pursuit had disappeared. As the platform slowly emptied of people, the disconsolate vicar was preparing to get onto the next train when he noticed something glinting on the floor. To his intense relief, he found it was his watch. Realising that the crowd would seriously impede his getaway, the pickpocket had evidently dropped the watch at his feet. The vicar's response had foiled this particular crime, but other victims of crime on the underground railway would not be so lucky.

At 11pm on 23 August 1880, 18-year-old Clarence Lewis waited on the platform of Kensington station. In his hand was a bag containing £105 in cash, the takings from his employer's shop in the West End, which the young man had been instructed to take back to the firm's office in Spitalfields. The train took some time to arrive and while Lewis was waiting, a young man named Henry Perry arrived on the platform. Lewis immediately recognised Perry as having previously worked for the same company. The pair chatted on the platform and, when the train arrived, Perry invited Lewis to share a first-class compartment with him.

The two lads boarded the train, making themselves comfortable in a plush empty carriage. However, as the train pulled out of the station, Perry's friendly demeanour suddenly changed. He pulled a bottle from his pocket and forced it to Lewis's mouth, commanding him to drink. When Lewis refused and pushed him off, he produced a cosh and began to viciously beat his former colleague about the head. A desperate fight ensued as Lewis came to the realisation that Perry was trying to kill him.

As the train hurtled through the dark tunnel, Perry opened the carriage door and tried to push his victim out onto the tracks. Although only semiconscious by this stage, Lewis summoned one last burst of strength. He pushed Perry back into the carriage and managed to drag himself under a seat for protection. Struggling to remain conscious, he lay still until he heard the train pulling into a station. Once it had ground to a halt, he tentatively pulled himself from under the seat and, finding the carriage empty, opened the door, falling out of the train onto the platform. As station staff rushed to his aid, Lewis managed to point out Perry before finally losing consciousness. The vicious thief was quickly arrested by railway officials and handed over to the police, who found the £105 Lewis had been carrying hidden in his jacket.

Clarence Lewis had suffered severe injuries during his frantic fight for survival. He was taken to hospital suffering from several lacerations to his head and painfully swollen hands, where he had tried to defend himself from his attacker's relentless blows. He spent 10 days in hospital and received treatment as an out patient for several weeks afterwards. Despite his horrific ordeal, however, he proved to be an excellent witness, remembering details of the assault and theft with sufficient calm and clarity to ensure his murderous assailant was found guilty. Henry Perry was sentenced to 20 years' penal servitude and 20 lashes with the 'cat o' nine tails' for his crime.

Terrifying ordeals such as that of Lewis were mercifully rare on London's underground railway. However, petty crimes such as pickpocketing and unruly or threatening behaviour continued to blight the network. As the century drew to a close, the situation seemed to be reaching crisis point.

In April 1890, a whole gang of miscreants who had been terrorising the underground network went up before the judge at Clerkenwell Sessions House. First to appear in the dock were George Crampton, 30, and William Turner, 21, accused of stealing a purse containing postal orders and 40 shillings belonging to a Mrs Smart. At the hearing, the victim related how she had been boarding a second-class carriage at Baker Street station when the two prisoners and a third man came up behind her and snatched the purse from her handbag. As soon as she got into the carriage, Mrs Smart realised what had happened and shouted to the guard to stop the train. Unfortunately, the train was already in motion, but Mrs Smart and the guard kept a close eye on the men as they ran down the platform, jumping into a third-class carriage as the train pulled out of the station.

The thieves spent an agonising few minutes as the train made its way through the tunnel, wondering whether Mrs Smart or the guard had got a good look at them. Unfortunately for them, both had. When the train pulled into the next station, the guard rushed from his post to grab Crampton and Turner. The third man managed to get away from the scene and disappear into the crowd.

At their trial, the two thieves were quickly found guilty and Mrs Smart listened in horror as their previous convictions were read out to the court. Crampton had four to his name while Turner had eight, including robbery with violence. Having heard quite enough about their nefarious careers, the judge sentenced Crampton to 16 months' imprisonment with hard labour and imposed a five-year prison sentence on Turner.

Later in the same sessions, 27-year-old Arthur Roberts was sentenced to 19 months' imprisonment with hard labour after being found guilty of stealing a lady's purse at South Kensington station. The unlucky thief had attempted to escape by jumping onto the tracks and climbing up onto the opposite platform, where he concealed himself behind an automatic weighing machine. His hiding place was quickly discovered by police and Roberts was arrested.

As the hearings continued, the judge began to lose his patience with the stream of underground railway thieves brought before him. After sentencing yet another pickpocket found guilty of stealing two purses at Farringdon station, he remarked that robberies were becoming so frequent on the railway that he would be forced to administer far more severe punishments in the future.

It appears the judge's threat went unheeded within the criminal fraternity. On 21 December 1898, a man who preferred not to be named for fear of reprisal wrote to *The Times*, relating a particularly unsettling story. He and his wife had been waiting for a train at Queens Road station when a large and rowdy gang suddenly appeared:

'Presently the train came in; then all at once these persons made a dead set on us as if they were making for the train. They hustled us and surrounded me, say a dozen men, feeling on my person for purse and watch; this latter they took with chain and locket attached to it. I kept struggling and shouting for porters but none came. Meantime, my wife had been pushed to the ground and the roughs looked for a necklace, but happily my wife had only black beads; she managed to scramble into a carriage, held the door until I joined her there, and only then came the guards. Where were the porters? Why were this lot of men, some 20 or 30, let on the platform? Somebody ought to have been in attendance. I ask you, Sir, whether this is not worse than highway robbery and assault of the darkest description, and this in the centre of civilised London at this day of the 19th century.'

While incidents such as that experienced by the couple at Queens Road were undoubtedly unsettling, the underground railway was occasionally the scene of darker crimes – though one of the worst was mercifully abortive. In October 1887, Arthur Horne, an 18-year-old printer's assistant from Clerkenwell, returned home unexpectedly one morning in a very agitated state of mind. His sister, Ida, watched worriedly as he removed something from a locked drawer in his room. When she asked what he was doing, Horne ignored her and left the house without uttering a word.

Soon afterwards, Horne met up with Matilda Horton, a girl with whom he had been romantically involved for around three months. Matilda was fond of Horne but had recently been worried by his erratic, overwrought behaviour. Her anxiety had grown the previous day when she thought she caught a glimpse of a pistol or revolver concealed in his jacket. However, when the two met up again the next morning Horne seemed to have calmed down, so she agreed to accompany him on an excursion to Westminster Bridge. Once there, he left Matilda gazing out over the Thames while he disappeared into a nearby jeweller's shop, returning some minutes later with an engagement ring.

Although she would never admit as much, it seems highly likely that Matilda rejected Horne's proposal. The young man's actions immediately after the purchase certainly suggest a spurned lover. After presenting Matilda with the ring, Horne took her to Westminster Tube station. He purchased two tickets and she presumed he was taking her home. When they got down to the platform, however, Horne suddenly jumped onto a train that was just departing, leaving her behind. Suddenly remembering the gun she thought she had seen the previous day, Matilda was struck with fear at what Horne might be planning. Filled with panic, she followed him on the next train.

An apprehensive journey ensued but, as her train pulled into Charing Cross station, to her great relief Matilda spotted Horne on the platform. She got out of the carriage and tried to calm the young man down. Before she had time to say a great deal, however, Horne produced the handgun from his pocket and started firing at her. Luckily, he was not a good shot. The bullet missed his girlfriend and lodged in the back of the seat on which she had been sitting. Then, a split second later, as incredulous travellers looked on in horror, Horne calmly put the barrel into his mouth and pulled the trigger.

After the police had cleared the platform of shocked passengers, they searched Arthur Horne's body in a bid to discover why he had tried to shoot his girlfriend before turning the gun on himself. Their worrying discovery indicated Horne may have been planning a scene of carnage that morning. In his pockets were no fewer than 40 cartridges, suggesting he had considered shooting not only himself but other people too (although perhaps not Matilda). A pocketbook was also found on the body, the last entry of which read: 'As a token of love and respect, I wish my watch to be given to Matilda, being a last request. I remain yours truly, A. Horne. And please be kind enough to give Matilda my silk handkerchief. Will find it in my best jacket pocket. Call at Mitchell's, 5 Dyers-buildings, for three days pay.'

This rather strange note gave a clue as to Horne's confused state of mind at the time of his suicide. His thoughts had obviously centred on Matilda, but he still had the presence of mind to note that he was owed money by his employer. At the inquest, it became clear that although Arthur Horne had a tendency to be hot-headed, he was not a violent man and, as far as his family knew, he and Matilda had not argued a great deal. However, as the hearing progressed, it became clear that Matilda had previously been engaged to another man and, although she swore she had not been two-timing Horne, she still wore her former fiancé's ring – much to Horne's annoyance. Sadly, it seems that unrequited love killed Arthur Horne.

The proliferation of pickpockets on the underground railway – combined with occasional serious crimes and tragedies such as the death of Arthur Horne – stretched the transport police to their limits. By the end of the 19th century, the Metropolitan Police were struggling to enforce law and order in a city where the population had doubled since the force's inception in 1829. It therefore seemed imperative that the transport police should radically rethink their role, to prevent the underground railway from becoming too dangerous for travellers. Pressure on the railway companies to improve their standards of policing led, in 1900, to the London, Brighton & South Coast Railway completely reorganising its police force. Over the next 20 years, all of the London railways would follow suit.

In 1921, the Railways Act resulted in the merger of the country's railway network. As a result, the numerous independent railway police forces combined and reorganised into four groups, each responsible for policing a combination of lines. Each group was subsequently split into divisions headed by a superintendent in charge of a team of inspectors, detectives and constables. Pay and working conditions were improved to attract better calibre employees, laying the foundations for today's British Transport Police. The new police forces were tasked with maintaining a more effective standard of law and order on the railways, while maintaining their old remit to watch over the safety of rail travellers. Over the following decades, this task would stretch the railway police to their limits.

CHAPTER 8

DANGER UNDERGROUND

Subterranean London has never been devoid of accidents. Prior to the 1860s, the sewers were the main danger zones, particularly when deadly gases built up in the narrow pipelines beneath the city streets. With no outlet, the gases reached pressures so great that they could cause immense explosions, wrecking nearby buildings in the blast. In the early part of the 19th century, however, much of subterranean London was largely unpopulated, restricting the injury or loss of life that might otherwise occur from any accidents. It was only when the Metropolitan Railway arrived that underground London suddenly became filled with people and there was a far greater corresponding risk.

One of the first major calamities to afflict the new railway occurred at Bishops Road station on 9 May 1864. The busy rush hour was beginning to subside as engine driver William Greaterley and stoker Thomas Mount prepared the 9.15am Metropolitan Railway train for departure. However, just as the train was about to pull out of the station, a massive explosion ripped through the engine, sending the boiler shooting up into the air. Staff watched incredulously as the heavy iron tank flew through the glass roof before rapidly descending. It landed some 200 yards away from the station, near the entrance to the Dudley Arms pub. Inside the station, passengers and staff groped through the smoke and steam in an attempt to escape, as hundreds of jagged glass shards rained down from the shattered windows. Passengers waiting in the train were showered with debris that shot through the carriages with force, causing some very nasty injuries.

As the blinding steam gradually cleared, the extent of damage caused by the explosion was revealed. Daylight shone through the gaping hole in the roof where the boiler had ripped through. Virtually all of the station's windows had been shattered by the force of the blast. Luckily, however, the people on the platforms had managed to shield themselves from injury behind walls and pillars. The passengers in the train's carriages were not so fortunate. They had not been able to escape the shrapnel as the train's windows blew in, many of them suffering severe cuts and bruises. Station staff hurriedly summoned cabs to take the injured to nearby St Mary's Hospital. Amazingly, both Greaterley and Mount escaped the blast with relatively minor wounds, although Mount was taken to the hospital for observation as he felt faint.

Although engine malfunction was by no means a rare occurrence during the early days of the underground railway, few incidents caused as much damage as the explosion at Bishops Road. Indeed, the Tube quickly developed a reputation as a very safe mode of transport for Londoners. Claustrophobic commuters who avoided descending into its subterranean tunnels faced a far greater risk of injury in the omnibuses fighting their way through the chaotic traffic above ground.

By the beginning of the 20th century, however, the sheer number of trains and passengers beneath the city streets prompted the railway companies to reconsider safety issues. One potential threat that had caused concern for many years was that of fire. There had never actually been a major conflagration on London's underground railway, but, in 1903, a terrible fire on the Paris Métro, in which 84 people lost their lives, forced Tube bosses to address how they would cope if such a fire raged under London.

A survey of the underground railway network was undertaken and new guidelines on how to reduce the risk issued to all railway companies in the capital. The report recommended all platforms should have access points at both ends to avoid bottlenecks, the tunnels should have greater ventilation, rolling stock should be constructed from non-flammable materials and overcrowding in the carriages should be kept to an absolute minimum. The tendency of some commuters to drop lit matches and cigars onto wooden carriage floors and platforms was also questioned. In the event, however, virtually none of the safety committee's suggestions were brought into effect on the grounds of expense. The railway companies simply crossed their fingers and hoped that a serious fire would never break out.

It was not the only threat that increased in the 20th century. The Victorian underground railway had seen amazingly few train collisions and the occasional crash rarely resulted in serious injury. However, as the number of trains on the network got larger, the antiquated signalling system that had been used for decades began to fail.

In March 1938, faulty signals caused two Northern Line trains to collide between Waterloo and Charing Cross stations injuring 12 passengers. Less than two months later, the signals outside Charing Cross failed once again and two District Line trains smashed into one another.

At around 10am on 17 May, automatic signals told the driver of a Barking-bound train to stop in a tunnel midway between Charing Cross and Temple stations. However, as the driver waited for the signal to resume the journey, the train behind him, which had not been given the signal to stop, came rushing through and ploughed into the waiting train, pushing the two end carriages up into the roof of the tunnel. The passengers in the second from last carriage of the stationary train fared the worst. Trapped in the wreckage, those most severely injured gradually slipped into unconsciousness as rescue teams frantically attempted to reach them. Eventually, the fire brigade found it necessary to cut through the sides of the most badly damaged part of the train. They finally got inside the twisted remains of the rear carriages after 2½ hours, by which time six people had succumbed to their injuries. Another 40 passengers suffered injuries severe enough for them to be taken to hospital.

Faulty signals were the cause of another horrific crash in April 1953, when two Central Line trains collided in a single-track tunnel between Stratford and Leyton in east London, killing 12 and injuring many more. At the subsequent inquiry, the driver of the front train, Mr A. T. Bryan, vividly described the events that led up to the fatal collision. Clearly still shaken, Mr Bryan explained that on reaching Stratford station on the night of the crash, he was told by a London Transport employee that the signal ahead had got stuck on 'danger' and that he should wait for one minute before proceeding, to make sure the tunnel was clear.

Bryan did as he had been instructed and then slowly pulled off into the tunnel. Almost immediately, he saw the tail light of a stationary train in front of him. Realising that the information he had been given at Stratford was incorrect and that the tunnel was not yet clear, Bryan telephoned his guard at the back of the train, telling him they could not proceed. Fearing that the following trains would be given the same instructions, he also instructed the guard to check that their tail lamp was burning. As soon as Bryan had issued this instruction, the train ahead began to move off. He picked up his telephone again to tell the guard, but had barely finished speaking when there was a terrific crash.

Mr Bryan immediately realised what had happened. Fearful of what he was about to find in the carriages behind him, he steeled himself, opened his door and began walking through compartments of shocked and bleeding passengers, doing his best to reassure them. As he continued further down the carriages, the carnage grew increasingly bad. He was driven on by concern for his passengers and his guard, who he knew had been at the back of the train when the crash occurred.

The worst damage in the crash had occurred in the second coach of the second train. On impact with Mr Bryan's stationary train, the sides of the carriage had burst and passengers inside had been thrown against the wall of the tunnel and crushed amid the wreckage. Twelve people lost their lives and several others were seriously injured. Amazingly, despite being right at the point of impact, Mr Bryan's guard escaped relatively unhurt.

Even when it was working properly, the underground railway's signalling system was not foolproof and vigilance on the part of the driver was often called for – especially on open sections of track in bad weather. On one foggy morning in December 1945, two trains had made their way along the open track of the Metropolitan Line's western reaches. Visibility in the thick 'pea souper' was extremely limited and danger signals along the track warned the drivers to proceed with great caution. At Northwood Hills, the front train stopped at a red signal and waited for the all-clear to move off. At this point the second train suddenly appeared out of the fog and slammed into its rear, telescoping two of the coaches, causing the internal electrical wiring to arc and burst into flames. The guard saw what was happening just in time and threw himself clear of the collision with seconds to spare. His passengers were not so lucky. Three people were killed and several others injured. It is likely the death toll would have been much higher if the trains had been in a tunnel at the time of collision.

A spate of post-war accidents caused by faulty signals prompted a major inspection of all signalling equipment on the underground railway. By the end of the 1950s, it was hoped that this dangerous problem had been resolved. However, it was at this time that another potentially fatal problem reared its head. At the time, much of the rolling stock on the underground railway was well over 30 years old. While age alone did not compromise the safety of the trains, the dated electrical wiring in some coaches was becoming a definite hazard.

In July 1958, one person on a Central Line train died and 49 fellow passengers were taken to hospital after the electrics short-circuited and caused a major fire. The train was in a tunnel between Shepherd's Bush and Holland Park stations in west London when a passenger suddenly noticed smoke drifting through the carriage. He quickly reached up and pulled the emergency alarm handle, stopping the train inside a tunnel where, unfortunately, the fire quickly began to take hold. As the air grew thick with noxious smoke, the terrified passengers jumped from the carriages and stumbled down the dark tunnel in search of a station. Thirty-seven of them found their way through the darkness back to Shepherd's Bush, which seemed to take forever before they glimpsed the lights of the platform. Staggering up into the station, they were ushered into the fresh air by waiting staff. As they collapsed onto the pavement outside, they learned to their dismay that had they walked in the opposite direction, they would have reached Holland Park station within 50 yards.

Two years later, passengers on another Central Line train had a lucky escape when an electrical fault caused smoke to billow into the carriages of a train bound for Gants Hill, in the east London/Essex suburbs. Luckily, the prompt, level-headed actions of driver Arthur Bishop and guard Felix Samuels resulted in all passengers escaping without injury. As passenger Geoffrey Deeley told *The Times*: 'Smoke was pouring into the carriages. We had to break the windows. The firemen formed a chain and helped the people through the train to the last carriage. The smoke was choking us and women were screaming.' Many other travellers praised Bishop and Samuels, who had remained on the train while they waited for the emergency services, going up and down the smoke-filled carriages to reassure their dazed and anxious passengers.

By the 1970s, improvements in signalling equipment and safer electrics on the Tube had greatly improved the safety of the trains. However, the last quarter of the 20th century was marred by accidents on the underground railway so shocking that they were reported across the globe. These horrific tragedies would change Londoners' perception of the Tube forever.

On Friday 28 February 1975, the 8.38 Highbury shuttle left Drayton Park on its short journey to Moorgate station, which lay just 3½ miles down the line. The route, then part of the Northern Line, was popular with commuters who travelled into the City from their homes in the suburbs of north London. That Friday, the commute began in much the same way as any other, the carriages gradually filling with people keen to get the day over with so that they could relax and enjoy the weekend. For some, however, it would be the last day of their lives.

As the train made its way down the line into the City, a few passengers adjusted themselves in their seats as carriages lurched from side to side. One of them, Mrs Frances Rhodes, later told the *Daily Express*, 'The train seemed to pull away more quickly than usual. I said to myself, "He's in a hurry."' Mrs Rhodes was not the only person on the train who noticed it was travelling faster than usual. As it approached its final stop at Moorgate it showed little sign of slowing down, prompting guard Robert Harris to comment to one of the passengers, 'What does he think he's playing at up front?' No sooner were the words out of his mouth than the train flew through the station and into a blind tunnel, from which there was no exit. Bryan Fryer, a Northern Line guard who was standing near the tunnel entrance, explained to the *Daily Mirror*: 'I didn't hear any braking. The red light at the front of the sand drag went flying and the sand went up in the air. I thought the train was going to mount the platform and I threw myself against the wall. There was sand in my ears, eyes and hair. I was flabbergasted.'

Relief signalman Walter Wade also watched as the train rushed past, thinking to himself, 'Christ, it's not going to stop!' In horror, Mr Wade looked on helplessly as a terrific crash emanated from the inside of the tunnel, followed by a heavy pall of thick black smoke. The train had careered at full speed into the wall at the end of the tunnel. The sheer brute force of the impact condensed the front carriage to half its original length. The passengers inside had been thrown forward like ragdolls, lying in a twisted heap that reached up to the ceiling. The second coach had slid under the first carriage's back wheels, lifting the wreck upwards, while the third coach had reared up over the second, jamming itself in a tiny space between the carriage roof and the ceiling of the tunnel. At this point, the short tunnel had become so packed with wreckage that the remaining three carriages had stopped along the station platform.

As station staff rushed the uninjured passengers from the back coaches out of the station, frantic calls were made to the emergency services. On arriving at the scene, medical staff and fire crews saw that they had an incredibly difficult task on their hands. They would have to summon every ounce of ingenuity and willpower to have any chance of rescuing survivors trapped in the tunnel wreckage. The three front coaches had wedged themselves so tightly into that space that pulling them out without causing even more damage was impossible. The only way to reach the people inside was to cut through the tangled mess of metal, wood and shattered glass section by section. A fire crew managed to break their way into the back of the third carriage, but, as they slowly made their way forward, they realised that the choking black smoke that billowed out of the train when it hit the wall had permeated every pocket of air. With little oxygen, work was laborious, stiflingly hot and dangerous. Coupled with the airless atmosphere was the dreadful fact that the crews were surrounded by the bodies of dead and dying passengers, which tested their resolve more than anything else in the hellish tunnel.

Inside, those passengers still alive listened in relief as the rescue team gradually edged closer to them. Policewoman Margaret Liles, one of the last to be freed, told a reporter from the *Mirror*, 'As soon as we saw the rescuers and heard their calm voices, there was an enormous sense of relief. There were bodies all around but I knew we would be safe. I just felt glad I was alive. I didn't mind what injuries I had.'

It took four days to clear the train wreckage from the tunnel. The relentless work of the rescue crew ensured that many victims of the crash were brought out of the tunnel just minutes before they would have suffocated in the airless atmosphere. Nevertheless, the crash claimed the lives of 43 people, making it the worst accident in the underground railway's history. The question remained, how on earth had it happened?

At first, many people assumed that the driver of the train, 55-year-old Leslie Newson, was to blame and had either suffered a severe lapse of concentration or else had decided to commit a very destructive public suicide. More charitable speculators thought the driver had probably suffered a paralysing stroke or heart attack immediately before the crash, resulting in the train running out of control. However, evidence at the inquest undermined both theories.

Following its retrieval from the crushed carriage, a full autopsy was carried out on Mr Newson's body. The pathologist found that the man had been very fit for his age and that there were absolutely no signs of cardiac arrest or stroke. In addition, every Tube train had been fitted with a 'dead man's handle' – a lever held by drivers while the trains were in motion. Should the driver suddenly be taken ill or faint, he would automatically lose his grip on the dead man's handle, which in turn would activate the brakes. Mr Newson did not do this.

It also seemed extremely unlikely that Newson had committed suicide. Colleagues and family members described him as a quiet, meticulous man who, although at times introspective, enjoyed a contented family life. At the time of the crash he had £300 with him, which he had agreed to loan his daughter so that she could buy a car. He had also made arrangements to help his brother-in-law paint his house over the coming weekend. These were hardly the actions of someone planning to commit suicide.

Eighteen-year-old Debbie Connolly also came forward to defend Mr Newson's character, telling the press how he had come to her rescue when she was being attacked on a train the previous summer. As she recalled, 'It was a terrifying experience. It was also a very nasty experience for Mr Newson ... He was so kind and a great comfort to me. I will always remember him as a hero.'

Leslie Newson's driving skills were brought into question briefly at the inquest when Robert Harris, the guard on the fated train, admitted that, a few days before the crash, the driver had overshot another station platform. When he later spoke to him about it, Newson apparently said, 'I misjudged it. I dropped the handle but it did not stop as quick as I thought.' However, Harris did not think the overshoot was serious enough to report and Raymond Deadman, who had trained Mr Newson, told the inquest, 'He tended to be rather cautious – one would say nervous – but at all times in the driver's cab, Mr Newson appeared very competent.'

Unable to apportion blame for the accident to the driver, the inquest looked at reports on the train itself but found there was nothing to suggest any catastrophic failure of brakes. Most mysteriously, witnesses on the platform at Moorgate that fateful morning reported seeing Mr Newson sitting bolt upright in the driver's compartment, staring straight ahead as the train hurtled past. If the brakes had failed, would he not have been wrestling with the controls in a desperate bid to make it stop?

Sadly, the only person who could have revealed the true reason behind the Moorgate train disaster – Leslie Newson – was dead. The jury returned a verdict of accidental death on the 43 victims, but what caused the accident remains a complete mystery to this day.

Following the accident, an automatic stopping system was introduced. Known as 'Moorgate Control', it triggered emergency brakes if a train entered a terminus station too quickly, in the hope of ensuring such a disaster never happened again.

As the controllers of London Underground worked to reassure their passengers that the Tube was still a safe method of transport, the old debate regarding smoking on the Underground once again came to the fore. The issue had divided Londoners ever since the underground railway came into existence. Smoking carriages on the Tube had long since been highly unpleasant places, even for people who smoked. The air reeked and, at rush hour, those who asserted their right to a cigarette blew fumes into the faces of those packed closely around them, causing more than a little consternation.

Frank Kendrick, a City worker who commuted on the Piccadilly Line every weekday throughout the 1970s and 80s, recalls, 'The smoking carriages on the Tube were disgusting but in rush hour you sometimes had no choice but to get into one. When I got home, my clothes reeked of stale tobacco and occasionally I even had my coat accidentally burned by cigarettes.' What bothered him even more were the smouldering dog-ends that littered the floor of the carriages. 'I often watched as people dropped lit cigarettes in the Tube,' he remembers. 'At the time the floors of the coaches were made from wooden slats and the dog-ends would roll into the ridges and burn away there until they reached the filter. Sometimes, they would also roll out of the carriage when the train stopped and fall onto the track. Although I'd never heard of a fire being caused by them, I always thought to myself, "That is really dangerous."'

Unfortunately, Kendrick's fears were justified. In 1980, red hot ash from a discarded cigarette blew into a tunnel at Goodge Street station, setting fire to a ventilation shaft that staff used as an unofficial storeroom. The resulting blaze sent suffocating smoke billowing through the tunnel to envelop the carriages of a passing train, choking the passengers inside with deadly carbon monoxide. Allan Williamson, a 56-year-old Edinburgh man, suffered a fatal heart attack after breathing in the toxic fumes.

Following the deadly fire, smoking was banned on all Tube trains. Although the ash that caused the conflagration may well have come from a cigarette smoked on the platform, London Transport declined to stop waiting passengers from lighting up. They also continued to allow smoking in all other areas of Tube stations, including the ticket office, corridors leading to platforms and escalators. This policy would ultimately prove deadly.

The dangers of smoking on the Tube were highlighted once again in November 1984, when a discarded match fell through a ventilation grille at Oxford Circus station and landed, still burning, inside a storeroom containing paint thinner and decorators' rags, causing a dangerous fire. The following morning, *The Times* reported: 'Hundreds of homeward-bound theatre-goers and sightseers were trapped in smoke-filled tunnels for nearly two hours last night as fire broke out in Oxford Circus Underground Station. Five trains were trapped by thick, black smoke billowing down tunnels. After the smoke dispersed, firemen found one train, which had been empty in a siding, destroyed and a system of tunnels at a crossing point of the Bakerloo and Victoria Lines totally burnt out; a section of platform badly damaged and three miles of tunnelling at Oxford Circus requiring extensive repairs. Tracks were buckled and hundreds of yards of cables burned through. A fire service spokesman said, "We have been very fortunate to have got away with so few injuries and no deaths."' Luckily, the fire had broken out at around 10pm, as the railway network was beginning to run down for the day. Had it started a few hours earlier, the aftermath might have been very different.

The Oxford Circus fire forced London Transport to issue a ban on smoking in all Underground stations. However, although the ban was adhered to on the platforms, many commuters took to lighting up as they made their way up the escalators. Thinking it pointless to stop this practice as the smokers were on their way out of the station, most staff chose to turn a blind eye to it. Little did anyone realise that this would soon have horrific consequences.

At around 7.20pm on 17 November 1987, a passenger on the up side of the Piccadilly escalator at King's Cross station lit up a cigarette and absentmindedly dropped the match at their feet. They had probably done this many times before and did not give their actions a second thought as they left the busy station. However, it inadvertently started a chain of events that would lead to the worst accident in the entire history of the underground railway.

What the passenger failed to realise was that the match had not gone out. Instead, it had fallen, still burning, through a gap in the escalator floor onto an inch-thick accumulation of grease, dust and debris. About eight minutes later, a passenger descending to the Piccadilly Line spotted smoke emanating from the up escalator and rushed to tell a ticket collector.

The emergency services were quickly alerted. Although the fire at this point did not appear that big, police decided that the best course of action would be to close the up escalator until the flames below it could be extinguished. Officers ran police tape across the bottom but tired commuters, keen to get home and unaware of the danger, pulled it off, ignoring pleas from station staff to use another exit. Up above them, a stream of people continued their descent on the down escalator whilst, beneath their feet, the flames grew higher.

By 7.40pm, the fire was beginning to get dangerously out of control. In a desperate bid to stop the steady stream of passengers, staff finally cut off power to the up escalator. With no sign of the fire brigade, a station inspector grabbed an extinguisher and entered the underside of the escalator, hoping to put it out. As he was driven back by the searing heat, flames reaching 5ft shot through the stairwell, drawn upwards by the oxygen above. Realising they had a major conflagration on their hands, King's Cross control room radioed the Piccadilly and Victoria Line trains en route to the station, telling them not to stop. In the meantime, passengers were still trying to push past staff and climb up the burning escalator.

To the relief of many, the fire brigade arrived just minutes after the inspector's failed attempt at putting out the fire. To the firefighters' intense frustration, however, they found that one of the fire hydrants had been blocked off by builders. Using what water was still available to them, they descended to the source of the fire as station staff and police evacuated passengers stranded on the Piccadilly Line platforms via the Victoria Line escalators – which, although unaffected by the fire, led to exactly the same area of the station as those of the Piccadilly Line.

By the time firefighters reached the source, the fire had taken hold of the old wooden escalator, fanned by sudden blasts of air caused by trains rushing past the station. As they battled to bring it under control and fleeing passengers spilled out into the ticket hall above, a massive fireball ripped from the burning staircase and raced up the escalator. Reaching the top, it engulfed the ticket hall in searing flames and flew down the Victoria Line escalator shaft, knocking people off their feet and setting their clothing alight. The actions of one careless passenger had turned King's Cross Underground station into an inferno.

The fireball caused mass panic. As the emergency services desperately tried to reach people trapped in the burning station, acrid black smoke invaded every space, making rescue almost impossible. One London Transport worker told the press, 'I was walking down the escalator when I suddenly saw a lot of smoke. Then I heard people screaming and shouting. It was horrific. Everyone started running up the stairs at me. I just had to run. It was awful … the worst thing I have seen in my life.' Other witnesses recalled the sudden emergence of the fireball as a 'sheet of flame' that shot across the ceiling of the station with shocking speed, igniting everything in its path. The passengers inside the booking hall did not stand a chance. Thirty-one people died and many others suffered agonising burns.

In the aftermath, an inquiry took a long, critical look at fire safety arrangements on the Tube and found them in a truly lamentable state. Despite guidelines being drawn up over 80 years previously, following the fire on the Paris Métro, virtually no measures had ever been implemented.

Tube stations did not have to comply with the same safety regulations as other public buildings. Consequently, at the time of the fire, they had no alarm system or recorded message to instruct passengers on evacuating the station. Neither were there any illuminated 'Emergency Exit' signs to lead disoriented passengers through the often warren-like tunnels to safety. Moreover, there was no sprinkler system in most booking halls and no smoke-proof doors in passageways to stop the deadly, fire-fuelling drafts caused by passing trains and no standard system of communication between Tube stations and emergency services. As the *Daily Mirror* commented after the tragedy, 'Any one of these measures – most of which are mandatory in public buildings elsewhere – might have saved lives in the King's Cross horror.'

London Transport took grave heed of the inquiry's findings. They promptly installed all Underground stations with sprinkler systems and heat detectors, rigorously enforcing a total ban on smoking. The old wooden escalators, many of which had been installed before World War 2, were replaced with metal versions. During the inquiry, it was discovered that the under-stair tracks of the Piccadilly Line escalators at King's Cross had not been cleaned since their installation in the 1940s. Consequently, there was a massive build-up of grease mixed with sweet wrappers, fluff, human hair and rat fur, lying inches away from passengers' feet. The inquiry recommended that all escalators be cleaned thoroughly at regular intervals to prevent such a conflagration ever occurring again.

The measures brought in following the King's Cross fire drastically improved safety for thousands of passengers on the underground railway. It was, needless to say, tragic that it took such a horror for safety measures to be finally implemented, many of which had been recommended decades previously. However, although the new safety controls were timely, they did little to protect the public from a threat that had already jeopardised the Tube for over 100 years – terrorism.

CHAPTER 9

TERROR ON THE UNDERGROUND

On the morning of 7 July 2005, Anne Barry was in the kitchen of her Maida Vale home when the phone rang. On the line was her old friend Diane Cooper. 'Something strange has happened on the Tube,' said Diane. 'Turn on your television.'

Anne dutifully did as she was instructed, to find the BBC reporting an incident in a Tube tunnel apparently caused by a power surge. Although she had been travelling on the Underground for decades, Anne had never heard of such a thing before. Having temporarily given up work to raise her children, she lived only a 10-minute walk from Edgware Road station – which had apparently become one of the epicentres of the unfolding disaster. As she watched the dishevelled, bloodied commuters emerging, Anne, like many thousands of other Londoners, felt that the true cause was being momentarily suppressed. Her fears were confirmed when pictures were broadcast of a bus that had exploded near Tavistock Square. This was no power surge. London was under attack.

As the city struggled to make sense of events that unfolded on the day subsequently known simply as 7/7, the underground railway became the focus of an investigation into terrorism. Sadly, it was by no means the first time that the Tube had been targeted for such purposes. In fact, it had a long history of terror attacks which began in the last quarter of the 19th century.

※

The first bombing campaign was launched against the underground railway on 30 October 1883, with two explosions in tunnels near Paddington and Charing Cross stations which injured 60 people. The bombs, hidden in bags, had been discreetly lowered out of passing trains into the tunnels some hours before.

Examination of the devices revealed they had actually been timed to go off during one of the underground railway's busiest periods, but their clocks were faulty. Consequently, the trains affected by the explosions were not as full as intended, but the bombs still succeeded in causing fear, confusion and injury.

William George, who was caught up in the Paddington explosion, told the press, 'The train was rather full. I was in the last carriage of the train. We passed along alright as far as Praed Street. Afterwards I heard an explosion something like the report of a cannon. I saw a flash and the lights in our carriage went out suddenly. For one moment I thought it was caused by the lamp in our carriage but the next moment I found myself scrambling among the other passengers. When I had collected myself, I removed from my head a piece of glass about an inch and a half in length.'

Corporal Warren of the 4th Queen's Own Hussars had also been travelling on the Paddington train and agreed that the blast sounded like cannon fire. He told *The Times*: 'I was struck by something which knocked me almost insensible and when the train arrived at the station I staggered across the platform. I remember nothing more, except that a soldier picked me up.'

Following the blasts, the police launched a frantic manhunt in a bid to catch the bombers. A £1,000 reward was offered for information leading to apprehension of the perpetrators, but officers already had their own idea about who was responsible. Their suspicions were reinforced when Mr Bowman, the stationmaster at Holborn, received a threatening letter claiming that Snow Hill tunnel would be the next target. Written (perhaps deliberately) in a barely legible scrawl, the missive was signed 'Sectary of Brotherhod' (sic).

This was the Irish Republican Brotherhood, a covert organisation dedicated to establishing Irish independence from Britain. Along with their Irish-American counterparts, Clan na Gael, the Brotherhood carried out a sustained bombing campaign against targets on the British mainland in the 1880s, wreaking havoc at Salford Barracks in 1881 and the Local Government Board offices in Whitehall in March 1883.

Realising they had little hope of catching the men who had planted the underground bombs, the police decided to go after individuals they suspected of being the ringleaders. One week after the bombings, Scotland Yard issued a notice offering a reward for information on the whereabouts of John McCafferty and William O'Riordan.

According to most sources, McCafferty was an Irish-American, born in Ohio in 1838. During the American Civil War, he joined the Confederate Army and rapidly climbed the ranks, eventually making captain. Immediately after the war, he intended to use his newfound military skills to support the Irish independence movement. In 1865, he travelled to Ireland with the intention of helping the ongoing Fenian insurrection, but was arrested while still aboard the boat and sent back to America. Undeterred, he made his way back across the Atlantic the following year, but was arrested some months later at Dublin Harbour after organising an arms robbery at Chester Castle. McCafferty was tried for high treason (implying that he may have been a British citizen at some point) and initially sentenced to death. However, his sentence was later commuted and, by the time of the underground bombings, his whereabouts were unknown.

The other police suspect, O'Riordan, was also nowhere to be found. In early December, police received a letter from him bearing a Paris postmark in which he denied any involvement with the recent bombings in London, claiming he was in Cork with his family when they occurred. With no firm leads, the police found it impossible to proceed with their investigation.

Although the police had failed to apprehend a single person involved in the bombings, no further devices were planted on the underground railway throughout the remaining months of 1883. However, on 27 February of the following year, staff at Victoria station were preparing to shut down for the night when a powerful bomb ripped through the booking office, waiting rooms and luggage depository, causing massive amounts of damage. Once again, the explosives had been left in a bag, but this time it had been placed in the left luggage depository. On examining the charred remains of the bomb, the police found it had been timed to go off at an earlier hour, when the station would have been much busier. Luckily, as with the two previous bombs, the timer on the device was faulty.

The explosion at Victoria station caused a state of high alert at all of London's underground and overground railway stations. Staff watched vigilantly for any suspicious characters amid the throngs of passengers, and all luggage left in station depositories was searched. At Ludgate Hill station, the staff pragmatically worked their way through numerous carpetbags, cases and packages until they came upon a large leather portmanteau, left at the station two days before the explosion at Victoria. Prising open the lock on the bag to examine the contents, they found several cakes of dynamite attached to a timing device, wrapped within some articles of clothing. The portmanteau was handed over to firearms specialists at Woolwich Arsenal, who chillingly discovered that although the timer had activated, the pistol that was supposed to light the fuse had failed. The busy station had narrowly avoided a lethal catastrophe.

On the same day as the deadly portmanteau was left at Ludgate Hill, a man giving his name as 'Mr Berry' left an almost identical bag at the luggage office in Paddington station. On examination, it was found to contain more dynamite neatly wrapped in a copy of the *New York Sun* newspaper, dated 6 February 1884. Once again, the device had failed to go off. A third portmanteau containing dynamite would be found in the cloak room at Charing Cross station.

Realising it could be the start of a sustained bombing campaign, police embarked on a race against time to catch the bombers before they struck again. Unfortunately, their enquiries at the station luggage offices yielded little useful information. The porters at Ludgate Hill and Charing Cross received numerous bags every day and could not remember what the depositors looked like. However, the booking porter at Paddington remembered that the mysterious Mr Berry had a very dark complexion and was around 5ft 6" tall, although he could not be certain he would recognise him again.

The police were also helped by a particularly observant maid, who called in at her local police station with an interesting story after the bomb exploded at Victoria. The maid worked at the Waverley Hotel in Great Portland Street and had become suspicious of two men who stayed from 20 February until the day after the explosion. Her interest had been piqued when she realised they spent a good deal of time in each other's rooms, although when they were in public in the hotel they pretended not to know each other. Galvanised by the maid's story, officers searched the hotel and found part of a flap detached from the portmanteau at Paddington station, along with a tray from a cashbox that had also been found in the bag. The whereabouts of the two shady guests, however, remained a mystery.

Despite the evidence at the Waverley Hotel and the vague description of 'Mr Berry', the trail soon went cold. As the following months passed without further incident, the alarm caused at London's stations slowly subsided. However, the bombers had not finished their campaign.

On 30 May, two boys were walking round Trafalgar Square when they noticed a black leather bag hidden under one of the lions at the foot of Nelson's Column. When it was opened by the police, they found cakes of Atlas Powder (a brand of gunpowder), a detonator and a fuse. The bag did not contain a timing device, which suggested that, as the previous timers had been faulty, the bomber intended to return to the site at some point to light the fuse by hand.

Relief at finding the Trafalgar Square bomb before it went off was short-lived. That very same evening the terrorists struck again, this time exploding bombs at a smart private house and a gentleman's club in St James's Square. Audaciously, they also planted a bomb at Scotland Yard, right under the noses of the men who were tracking them. The resulting blast caused considerable damage to the CID and Special Irish Branch offices.

Humiliated by the bombers' impudence and fearful that more bombs would be planted, the police stepped up their search. Frustratingly, they failed to uncover a single clue to the identity of the attackers. However, as the US newspaper found in the bag at Paddington suggested links to Clan na Gael, Scotland Yard resolved to watch any Irish-Americans arriving in London very closely indeed.

On 2 January 1885, Hyde Park Constable John Seward was about to board a Metropolitan Line train at Bishopsgate station when a swarthy young man, who he presumed to be a guard, leaned out of one of the carriages and asked for a light. Seward lit a match for him and then got into an adjacent carriage, thinking no more of the encounter. However, as the train was passing through a tunnel just outside Gower Street station, a huge explosion rocked the train, extinguishing the lights and shattering the windowpanes. The Irish bombers had struck again – but this time, one of them had made a huge mistake. In a moment of hubris, he had foolishly made himself known to a policeman.

In the immediate aftermath of the Gower Street bombing, the police were still unaware that the man responsible had spoken to Constable Seward. However, time was about to run out for the foolhardy bomber.

On Saturday 24 January, two friends named Ann Nunn and Elizabeth Bailey decided to have a day out at the Tower of London. The women met at 1pm and made their way into the castle grounds. After visiting the famous jewel room and the ancient White Tower, they went into the chapel. Ann later described what happened next:

'There was no one in the chapel except two boys and a warder. We went out of the chapel and into the Banqueting Hall. The boys were in front of us. As we turned the corner we saw a little smoke coming up from the right; it seemed to be coming from the floor. After that there was a dreadful noise and it seemed as if I was being driven back.'

Ann and Elizabeth had unwittingly walked straight into a bombing. The explosion knocked them off their feet and sent a display of rifles toppling onto them. Ann was badly injured and had to remain in hospital for over a week.

One of the boys, Ernest Stratton, was also badly hurt and hospitalised for several days. His companion, Herbert George, described what happened in the banqueting hall:

'I noticed some smoke and a smell like gunpowder. Then about three minutes after there was an explosion and I think I was knocked down. I was hurt on my thigh and right hand.'

The immediate aftermath threw the Tower onto red alert. Staff acted quickly, closing all gates before any of the visitors could leave. The police rapidly arrived on the scene and everyone inside was compelled to satisfy them with their reason for being there. Although all those questioned were understandably shaken, one dark-haired man seemed particularly nervous. As police asked what had brought him to the Tower that morning, they noticed he kept repeating their questions as if buying himself a few seconds to think up a plausible alibi. He told them his name was James George Gilbert and that until very recently he had been employed at the Liverpool docks. Unconvinced by his story, the police quickly telegrammed the dock master at Liverpool, who had no record of a James George Gilbert. Suspecting they may well have got their man, the police arrested 'Gilbert' who, on being remanded into custody, revealed his real name was John Cunningham.

The police lost no time in visiting Cunningham's lodgings to look for incriminating evidence. Finding surprisingly little in his room and establishing with his landlady that he had also given her a false name, they went to an address where Cunningham lodged previously at Great Prescott Street in Whitechapel. The landlady of this establishment was much more helpful. She told police that Cunningham had arrived at the house with a large trunk which, shortly before he left, had been taken away in a cab by another man. The police managed to track down the cab driver who transported the large trunk and he remembered taking it to 90 Turners Road in Bow, the residence of one Harry Burton – a cabinetmaker who spent much of his time in America. Officers waited for Burton to return home from work and arrested him.

It transpired that both Burton and Cunningham had been heavily involved in terrorism on the British mainland since early 1884. On 20 February of that year, Burton had arrived in England with an unknown man aboard the SS *Donau*. During the voyage he told fellow passengers he had come to England looking for work, but in fact he had a much more malicious plan. Once the ship had docked in Southampton, Burton immediately ventured into town and purchased two portmanteaus from local retailers. These two leather bags were later used to conceal the abortive station bombs.

Immediately after the bombing of Victoria station, Burton and his anonymous accomplice had boarded a ship back to the USA. He returned to Britain on 24 May, however, taking lodgings at Limehouse and finding employment with a local cabinetmaker. Shortly after the bombings on 30 May, he left England once again, telling his landlady he had to go back to America to vote in the presidential election. Just before Christmas, he returned and made contact with Cunningham, who was also in Britain by this time. As police pieced together the evidence, they called Constable Seward, who had been on the bombed Gower Street train, to check whether he recognised either Cunningham or Burton. Seward immediately pointed Cunningham out in a line-up as the man who had asked him for a light.

With the weight of evidence stacked against them, Cunningham and Burton were found guilty of causing explosions at various locations during 1884-85 and sentenced to life imprisonment. However, their capture was a small victory for the police in a war on terrorism that would challenge them continually over the next 100 years, running all the way into the 21st century. Although two bombers had been captured, dozens more had evaded arrest. The men seen at the Waverley Hotel were never brought to justice. Neither was Burton's travelling companion, nor the men responsible for the bombs at Paddington and Charing Cross in 1883.

The Irish republican movement was a shadily enigmatic web of committed, ruthless men and women with no reservations about killing or maiming innocent people to further their cause. The incarceration of Cunningham and Burton barely affected their campaign. Over the next 50 years, the republicans continued their fight for independence. As their support grew, a rebel militia was formed which, after the Easter Rising of 1916, became known as the Irish Republican Army – or IRA. At first, the IRA concentrated their campaign upon Ireland. However, in 1939 they briefly turned their attention back to London and its underground railway.

On 4 February 1939, two large suitcase bombs planted by IRA operatives exploded at Tottenham Court Road and Leicester Square Underground stations, causing widespread damage and panic. Later that year, a further two devices exploded at King's Cross and Victoria stations, killing one man and injuring numerous others. However, this particular campaign receded quickly as events in Europe temporarily overshadowed the Irish republican cause. Things remained quiet in the aftermath of World War 2, but, by the closing years of the 1960s, the IRA was once again laying plans to inflict terror on the Underground.

On 23 August 1973, railwayman Mr L. Mylam was walking through the Bakerloo Line booking office at Baker Street when he noticed a plastic carrier bag printed with a Union Jack, propped up against the plate-glass window of a chemist's shop. Thinking the bag had been accidentally left there by a tourist, Mr Mylam bent down and peered inside. To his horror, he saw two wires leading from a battery to a small clock. He called the stationmaster and an evacuation of Baker Street station began.

The bomb was successfully defused by bomb squad officer Peter Gurney, who found that it had been timed to go off at 5.40pm – when the station would have been full of rush-hour commuters. Following the discovery, staff at Baker Street and several other Underground stations received anonymous telephone calls warning that further explosive devices were about to detonate. The resulting evacuation caused chaos. Thousands of travellers were barricaded out of the stations as police searched for the devices, but no more bombs were discovered. Eventually, all Underground stations were reopened and weary commuters travelled home unaware that these incidents were just the start of a disruptive assault on London by active IRA cells.

Over the following week, no fewer than 26 IRA bombs were found in London. The first wave of devices were hidden in cigarette packets and left in major West End stores including Harrods, Liberty and Austin Reed. Next was a series of letter bombs addressed to specific individuals. Most were discovered before they exploded but one did go off at the Stock Exchange, injuring the unfortunate secretary who opened it. The letter bombs were swiftly followed by more devices left in carrier bags.

As the bomb squad struggled to cope, another device was discovered at Baker Street station. A Woolworth's bag containing 1¾lb of gelignite attached to an alarm clock was found on the footbridge connecting the two Metropolitan Line platforms, close to the staff offices and canteen. Luckily, the device was discovered by a signal engineer who accidentally hit the bag with his briefcase whilst crossing the footbridge. The station manager quickly evacuated the platforms below and services on the Metropolitan Line were suspended as staff carefully placed a wooden shed around the bag, in an attempt to contain the blast should the bomb explode.

This second Baker Street bomb was also successfully defused by a bomb squad officer, but no sooner had the police begun to let passengers back into the station than a coded warning was received that another device had been planted at Marble Arch. Officers raced to the site and began evacuating the area. By this time, it was late at night and guests at the adjacent Cumberland Hotel were turned out on the street in their nightclothes while the area was searched. The police began a frantic hunt for the bomb but, this time, they were too late. The resulting blast ripped through the western end of Oxford Street, shattering the windows of nearby buildings. The explosion could be heard over two miles away.

The disruption caused by the Marble Arch bomb encouraged the IRA to continue with their campaign into the latter months of 1973. On 11 September, 13 people were injured when bombs exploded at King's Cross and Euston mainline stations. As Christmas approached, families hoping to take their children on annual shopping trips to the West End began to question the sanity of venturing into an area that was the IRA's number one target. The IRA had created a highly effective campaign of 'bomb and bluff' and it was impossible to guess where they were going to strike next. While the police kept a vigilant eye on the capital's busy shopping streets, the bombers turned their attention to pubs. The Tube was also targeted again when a device left in a telephone box at Sloane Square station exploded. Luckily, no one was injured in that particular blast, but, during Christmas 1973, a total of 24 bombs injured 73 Londoners.

The following year saw devices explode at the Boat Show in Earl's Court and Madame Tussaud's waxwork exhibition. The Christmas shopping season was once again disrupted by explosions, including a car bomb outside Selfridges and an explosion at Harrods.

In 1975 it was not much quieter. Following a sustained campaign across the British mainland, the IRA once again turned their attentions to London's underground railway. In October, Piccadilly was rocked by an explosion at Green Park Underground station, which killed one man and injured 18 other commuters. The bomb, left in a bag at a bus stop just outside the station, caused massive damage. Rosina Kemmett, 25, who was standing feet away from the explosion, told the press, 'There was a flash and a large bang. It seemed to come from the centre of the road. I got a mouthful of dust and bits, and although I was very dazed, I staggered to The Ritz and called the police before being treated.'

Lenny Ping had been driving his minicab down Piccadilly when the device went off, describing the scene thus: 'There was glass falling from a car showroom and a taxi passing the Tube station had its roof caved in by the blast. I saw a girl lying motionless on the pavement on the other side of the road. Her legs were covered in blood.'

The bomb caused serious damage to the surrounding buildings. Glass in the swing doors of the nearby Ritz Hotel was shattered and a porter from *Le Coq*

D'Or restaurant in Stratton Street described to the press how he was blown off his feet by the blast. A woman dining in the same restaurant described the moment the bomb exploded rather more nonchalantly: 'The building went up and down and we felt the tremor. Windows alongside the restaurant were blown in but the curtains were drawn and no one was injured.'

Despite the campaign of terror being waged against them, most Londoners took the bombings entirely in their stride. Another diner at *Le Coq D'Or* summed up the attitude of many when he told the press that, once the bomb had exploded, 'we carried on eating and drinking because there seemed no point in doing anything else.'

One of the key characteristics of the Irish republican campaign of terror was the anonymity of its perpetrators. From the early days of Clan na Gael right through to the 1970s, the majority of the men or women who planted the bombs had no criminal record and so were almost impossible to track down. In addition, the political motivation behind the bombings ensured that any arrests made were controversial.

The inability to put a stop to the IRA's activities frustrated the British government. As a result, the treatment of any individuals that were apprehended was tainted by the suspicion and paranoia felt by the authorities. Convicted IRA members were often subjected to 'special treatment' in prison, including solitary confinement, the strip searching of visitors and refused repatriation to prisons in Ireland. These practices sometimes had fatal consequences.

In 1973, Irishman Frank Stagg was convicted at Birmingham Crown Court of possessing 'articles with intent to destroy property' which the police suspected were to be used in a bombing campaign targeting Coventry. Stagg was sentenced to 10 years and sent to the high-security Albany prison on the Isle of Wight. From there, he was transferred to HMP Parkhurst in March 1974, where he and fellow republican Michael Gaughan went on hunger strike in support of IRA activists Dolours and Marion Price – then on hunger strike in London's Brixton prison in a fight to obtain political prisoner status.

At the time, hunger strikes were dealt with brutally by prison authorities who force-fed prisoners by ramming tubes down their throats. Gaughan's brother John visited him while he was on hunger strike and was shocked at what he saw. He later revealed that his brother's 'throat had been badly cut by force feeding and his teeth loosened. His eyes were sunken, his cheeks hollow and his mouth was gaping open. He weighed about six stone.'

The warders' violent attempts at force-feeding Gaughan ultimately proved futile. He died on 3 June 1974, aged just 24. Following his death, the Price sisters were granted repatriation but Stagg's requests to be moved to an Irish jail fell on deaf ears. Instead, he was transferred to Long Lartin Prison in Worcestershire and placed under close surveillance. Incensed, Stagg declared himself a political prisoner and refused to do any work. As punishment, he was placed in solitary confinement and consequently went on hunger strike in protest, until the prison governor gave assurance that neither he nor his visitors would be strip-searched any longer.

In 1975, Stagg was transferred again, this time to HMP Wakefield. Almost immediately, he embarked on another hunger strike to gain repatriation for himself and several other IRA prisoners. By this time, prolonged malnutrition had dangerously weakened his body and, after 62 days, he was dead.

Frank Stagg's death caused fury within the Irish republican movement. Plans were laid for vengeance. The day after he died, a 20lb bomb hidden in a case was discovered at Oxford Circus station. Intelligence collated by MI5 prompted the police to keep the Tube network under close surveillance, as it was certain that further attacks were being planned. Londoners were asked to be extra vigilant and to report any suspicious packages or bags to London Transport staff.

In this atmosphere of paranoia, the ordinary people of London continued to go about their business, putting the threat of bombings to the back of their minds. Roger France, who commuted on the Northern Line during the troubled 1970s, recalls how they took the IRA's threats in their stride: 'I can't remember anyone stopping using the Tube, although we were aware that the IRA could strike at any time.' Marjorie Watson, who worked as a secretary in Clerkenwell, agrees. 'I was always under the impression that the IRA warned stations to evacuate if they had planted a bomb, so – perhaps stupidly – I never worried about getting caught in any explosions.' Unfortunately, Marjorie's belief that bombers always gave warning of imminent explosions was not altogether correct. In fact, some of the IRA's actions did not go according to plan.

On the evening of 15 March 1976, the 4.34 Metropolitan Line train from Barking to Hammersmith was pulling out of West Ham station when a holdall belonging to a man in one of the carriages suddenly began to emit thick smoke. In panic, the man threw the bag down to the end of the compartment. It exploded with such force that it ripped the roof of the train open, showering the bomber and the passengers with shards of glass and lacerating strips of metal.

Shocked by the sounds of an explosion, the driver, 34-year-old Julius Steven, hastily brought the train to a halt and jumped out of his cab. He found a scene of devastation. Smoke poured from one carriage and the platform was covered with debris. As Mr Steven rushed down the train, the bomber suddenly appeared before him, frantically wielding a revolver. The brave train driver tried to make a grab for the man but, in the ensuing struggle, he was shot and mortally wounded.

By this time, station staff had alerted the emergency services. Whilst ambulance crews raced down to the platform to tend the injured, police officers went in search of the bomber. They found him trapped in a goods yard adjacent to the station. Realising he was cornered, he turned the gun on himself, screaming, 'You English bastards!', and pulled the trigger.

Julius Steven's death was thankfully not in vain. The bomber failed to kill himself, only inflicting a wound when he fired the gun, and his arrest led to the apprehension of two other members of an IRA active service unit, responsible for planting 16 bombs over a period of just six weeks. Their subsequent trial would reveal just how blindly committed these men were to their cause.

On 30 June, Julius Steven's killer – 36-year-old Adrian Vincent Donnelly, then a resident of Brixton– stood in the dock at London's Central Criminal Court, accused of conspiring to cause explosions. With him were John Hayes, 26, of Lavender Hill, and Patrick Hackett, 27, of Clapham Common. Hackett appeared in a wheelchair as he was recovering from his leg and hand being amputated, after a bomb he was carrying went off unexpectedly.

The three defiant men refused to recognise the court and appeared unmoved by the prospect of losing their freedom. The prosecution presented numerous pieces of evidence relating to how they had been making and planting bombs on a chillingly regular basis. Hayes and Hackett were sentenced to 20 years' imprisonment before the judge turned his attention to Donnelly, coldly telling him, 'I have looked in vain throughout this case for the least sign that you had any respect for human life … You seem to regard human life to be taken as easily as lighting a cigarette. You are a dangerous man and it is right that you should be removed from public life and from contact with human beings for as long as possible.' Donnelly was sentenced to life imprisonment with a recommendation that he spend at least 30 years in jail.

Throughout the remaining years of the 1970s and into the following decade, the IRA and other republican groups continued to create chaos on the British mainland. In London, they turned their attention toward above-ground targets. In March 1979, Shadow Northern Ireland Secretary Airey Neave was killed outside the House of Commons when the Irish National Liberation Army planted a bomb under his car. On 10 October 1981, two people were killed and 39 injured when a bomb hidden close to Chelsea Barracks exploded. Nine months later, two IRA bombs planted in Hyde Park and Regent's Park killed 11 members of the Royal Green Jackets and the Household Cavalry.

As republican bombers continued their deadly assault on London, their incarcerated compatriots continued to fight for political prisoner status. A series of headline-grabbing demonstrations were organised which included 'blanket protests', during which inmates wrapped themselves in bedding rather than wear prison uniforms, and 'dirty protests', where excrement was smeared onto walls by prisoners refusing to 'slop out' their cells. These demonstrations gradually escalated and ultimately led to a largely futile hunger strike at the notorious Maze Prison near Belfast in 1981, during which nine men starved to death. The strike was eventually called off after it became clear that the British government was not going to capitulate to the hunger strikers' demands. However, it did succeed in garnering international sympathy and support for the republican cause.

By the early 1980s, the rise of the republican political party Sinn Féin, coupled with the grim prospect of a seemingly never-ending death toll of innocents, finally persuaded the government to sign an agreement allowing the Irish Republic greater influence in the running of Northern Ireland. However, it stopped short of handing over complete control, stating that the Northern Counties would remain part of the UK for as long as the majority of inhabitants wished it. Unfortunately, this proved unacceptable to Sinn Féin and the IRA. The war was far from over. By 1990, republican cells were back in London, laying plans for a terror campaign in which the underground railway would play a major role.

During the summer of 1991, bombers began planting incendiary devices under the seats of Tube trains. These were not large enough to cause widespread damage, but the threat was enough to create chaos on the Underground network. Following the wave of firebombs, the IRA embarked on another series of hoaxes interspersed with real bombs. This wicked mix proved highly effective in throwing London into disarray and fuelled the strategy of a nationwide campaign – until a precarious peace was achieved with the Good Friday Agreement of 1998.

The end of the IRA's bombing campaigns was greeted with relief by Londoners, who looked forward to travelling about the city untroubled by the threat of explosions. However, this was not to last. On 7 July 2005, London's underground railway was rocked by the worst incident in its long history when extreme Islamists went on a suicide mission, exploding bombs on trains between Aldgate and Liverpool Street, Russell Square and King's Cross, and Edgware Road and Paddington. A bomb was also detonated on a bus at Tavistock Square. Fifty-two commuters died in the outrage and over 700 were injured.

Three of the bombers – Mohammad Sidique Khan, Shehzad Tanweer and Hasib Hussain – had travelled from Leeds to Luton to meet with their fourth compatriot, Germaine Lindsay, early that morning, taking the 7.25 train to King's Cross. Once there, CCTV footage showed the men hugging each other before saying goodbye and disappearing into the Tube network. Within minutes, they had caused utter chaos and carnage on the underground railway.

Tanweer and Khan both got onto Circle Line trains travelling in opposite directions. Tanweer boarded the second carriage of a train heading eastwards, placing a bag containing a bomb on the floor at his feet. Soon after the train had left Liverpool Street station, the device exploded. Scott Wenbourne, who was travelling in the third coach of the train, later told the *Daily Mirror* of the horror that unfolded before him:

'All of a sudden there was a loud bang and a flash of bright light. As soon as I hit the floor my first thought was, "It's a bomb." One of the train staff came along and said we had hit something but there was no need to panic. As we walked past the carriage we saw debris and torn metal. I noticed the carriage was completely ripped apart on one side … I saw three bodies on the track. I couldn't look, it was horrific. Many people had black faces, bleeding from parts all over their bodies.'

Seconds after the explosion in the tunnel at Liverpool Street, Khan's bomb, also on the floor of the second carriage, detonated with force as the train pulled out of Edgware Road station. Debris from the wreckage flew across the tracks, showering an eastbound train pulling into the station. Its driver, Jeff Porter, told the BBC: 'There was a train at the platform in front of me, coming the other way. As the driver's cab was just passing mine, I saw a bright yellow light on the train on the other side. It was like it happened in slow motion in my mind. As the other train passed me, my windscreen shattered. There was smoke and dust everywhere.'

Throughout the ensuing confusion, Mr Porter retained the presence of mind to oversee the evacuation of his passengers. He checked that the power had been cut to the train lines before guiding the shocked commuters through the train to his cab so that they could get out of the station, safely avoiding the centre of the devastation.

Workers at local businesses along the Edgware Road also rushed to help in the immediate aftermath. As rescuer Paul Dadge recalled: 'Staff from a nearby Marks & Spencer helped and we took the injured into the Metropole Hotel [opposite the station entrance] … It was quite surreal in a way, because in the Metropole there were people having business meetings who didn't know what had happened. We just said, "You have got to clear out so we can treat these people."'

As the Circle Line descended into chaos, a Piccadilly Line train raced through the tunnel connecting King's Cross and Russell Square stations. Among the crowds of commuters was the third bomber, Lindsay. His device exploded shortly after the train left King's Cross. Angelo Power, who was travelling in the doomed train, told a *Daily Mirror* journalist:

'There was a large bang. People were thrown out of their seats. Smoke immediately began to fill the carriages and people screamed because they thought they were going to die. Some began trying to break windows with their bare hands to try to get some air into the carriages because there was so much dense smoke. It was pitch black and there was total confusion … Eventually somebody at the back of the carriage managed to open the door but people were afraid to leave the train for fear of being electrocuted. We were all packed like sardines, waiting to die. I thought my time was up and so did everyone else. After about half an hour two policemen arrived … and started to lead people out. As I walked through the train I saw many people hurt and terrified.'

News of the explosions quickly began to filter through to the media. Estate agent John King was preparing to leave for work in Docklands when Radio London reported there was a major problem with the Tube. As he recalls, 'The radio announcer kept mentioning a power surge but I had never heard of such a thing causing an explosion before and something didn't quite add up to me.' As John listened to the radio, eyewitnesses began calling in to describe the carnage they had witnessed. Their descriptions convinced him that an electrical fault was not to blame. 'I couldn't believe that the authorities were sticking to the "power surge" theory when Radio London had tens of witnesses clearly describing the aftermath of a bomb.'

By 10am, this theory was confirmed as the transport authorities' cover story by the National Grid, which stated that no major problems had been reported that morning. Two minutes later, Scotland Yard officially announced that there had been a 'major incident' on the Underground system.

The 'incident' turned out to be the worst act of terrorism ever committed on British soil. With the city thrown into chaos and brought to a virtual halt, its visibly shocked mayor, Ken Livingstone, made an impassioned speech to rally Londoners. He addressed the bombers' sympathisers and collaborators: 'I say to those who planned this dreadful attack ... watch next week as we bury our dead and mourn them. But see also, in those same days, new people coming to this city to make it their home, calling themselves Londoners and doing it because of that freedom [the city offers] to be themselves.'

To many, the motivation for the bombings was difficult to comprehend. In the days that followed, there was much speculation as to why a group of young men would wish to kill both themselves and many others. However, the videotapes recorded by two of the men shortly before they died revealed their motivation to be largely political (while dressed in the trappings of religion).

On 1 September 2005, the Arab news channel Al Jazeera posthumously broadcast the tape made by Mohammad Sidique Khan. 'Our drive and motivation doesn't come from tangible commodities that this world has to offer,' said Khan. 'Your democratically elected governments continually perpetrate atrocities against my people all over the world. And your support of them makes you directly responsible, just as I am directly responsible for protecting and avenging my Muslim brothers and sisters.'

Whatever the reasons behind the bombings, it transpired that Livingstone had not overestimated London. In the days following the outrage, the city got back on its feet and its people continued to live, work and enjoy themselves. The metropolis was bloodied but remained unbowed.

CHAPTER 10

THE POST-WAR UNDERGROUND

London retains its position as one of the most heavily populated cities in the world. The sheer numbers of people living and working in the capital, combined with the demands of modern technology, have also ensured that by the dawn of the 21st century, underground London had become an intricate labyrinth of pipes, tunnels and cables.

Back in the 1860s, as the iron tracks of the railways were beginning to snake their way out of the capital, the population of Greater London was just three million, with very few people commuting into the city from its outer reaches. However, as the railways revolutionised travel and the movement of goods, the city exploded. By 1881, almost five million people were living in London. By the time the 1911 census was taken, the city had over seven million inhabitants and previously rural Middlesex villages such as Finchley, Hendon and Stanmore had been subsumed into the ever-expanding London boroughs.

London continued to grow through the disruption of the Great War. Although population figures took a slight dip during World War 2, by 1951 the capital was at its most crowded, with just over eight million people residing within its massively broad environs.

In addition to the millions who lived there, London also had to cope with thousands of commuters travelling into the city every weekday and a growing number of tourists who came to explore the capital, particularly in the summer months. The vast numbers of people put a huge strain on London's underground resources. Bazalgette's sewer system coped amazingly well, as more and more suburban branch pipes were connected to his colossal subterranean network, but elsewhere beneath the city, resources were beginning to feel the strain. Roads were constantly dug up to lay miles of new telephone and electricity cables; on the Underground railway, train carriages became claustrophobically crowded. The Tube network was subjected to the severest overcrowding as the

Piccadilly Line, in particular, struggled to cope with the thousands of workers it conveyed in and out of the city.

In 1948, as London was rebuilding itself after Hitler's bombing campaign, the British Transport Commission set up a working party to solve the problem of chronic overcrowding on the Underground. After much discussion, they came up with a proposal for a new Underground line to run from Walthamstow, in north-east London, through the West End to a terminus at Victoria station.

Despite the fact that a new Tube line was desperately required, it took years for the various Bills allowing construction to pass through Parliament, due to how the new tunnels would have to weave their way through the most densely packed subterranean soil in Britain. While the problematic route was slowly being worked out, the new railway was simply referred to as 'Route C'. As plans edged closer to completion, however, more inspiring names were put forward. The 'Viking Line' was suggested, an amalgamation of two key stations along the proposed route – Victoria and King's Cross. Similarly, the names of the two termini were combined to produce the less catchy 'Walvic Line'. Both were ultimately rejected in favour of the Victoria Line and work on the new railway began in 1962.

In order for the new Tube line to relieve congestion on the central London network, all Victoria Line stations (with the exception of Pimlico on the later Victoria to Brixton extension) would serve as interchanges with existing underground and overground routes. The first section of the line to be completed – Walthamstow to Highbury – opened to much excitement from railway enthusiasts on Sunday 1 September 1968. At 7.32am, driver William Harvey took the first train out of Walthamstow Central station on its maiden journey, its carriages packed with around 500 people who had queued for hours to ride on the first new Tube line built in London for 60 years. In one of the carriages sat retired sea captain Harold Coombes, who had travelled from his home in Norfolk for the opening ceremony. Captain Coombes was unique among the passengers that day. Back in 1906, when he was just 13 years old, he had ridden in the first Piccadilly Line train to make its way beneath London's streets. Although he was now 75, the Captain considered the opening of the Victoria Line just as exciting.

The Victoria Line proved an instant success. In December 1968, the section of track between Highbury and Warren Street opened. By 1971, the line was running right through the centre of London to Brixton. Its immediate popularity galvanised London Transport into resurrecting plans for another new underground railway. Provisionally named the 'Fleet Line' in deference to the ancient river, this subterranean railway would run at right angles to the Victoria Line's central section, connecting Baker Street with the City via Bond Street, Green Park, the Strand, Aldwych, Ludgate Circus, Cannon Street and Fenchurch Street, before turning southwards and running under the Thames into the south-east London suburbs.

Although the Fleet Line was a good idea, London Transport was aware that it would prove difficult to raise the funds necessary for construction. It was thus cannily decided to build the new railway in stages, spreading the cost over a number of years. The first phase began in 1971, when a branch of the Bakerloo Line running to Stanmore was extended from Baker Street, through Bond Street and Green Park, to a new terminus at Charing Cross. Construction of the tunnel proved slow and laborious. While the works plodded on, doubts were also raised about the suitability of the new line's name. Many people involved with the project felt the name 'Fleet' was inappropriate, as the route of the railway bore virtually no relation to the course of the Fleet River. As the works coincided with preparations for Queen Elizabeth's Silver Jubilee, it was decided that the railway should be renamed the Jubilee Line. Unfortunately, as it transpired, the name Jubilee would be no more appropriate when the line opened in 1979 – two years after the royal celebrations had finished.

It was originally intended that a second phase of construction on the Jubilee Line would extend the railway eastwards to a terminus at Fenchurch Street. Following the completion of this section, a third phase would take the line under the Thames to New Cross, while the final phase would extend it all the way to Bromley in the Kent suburbs. However, the painfully slow progress of the first phase, coupled with problems in obtaining further finance, kept the Jubilee Line extensions on ice until the late 1980s. By this stage, some of the areas through which the line was set to travel had changed beyond recognition. The Isle of Dogs, which had been ignored in the original plans, was rapidly becoming a major financial centre and desperately needed a Tube line. Consequently, the old route was scrapped, the old terminus at Charing Cross dispensed with and the line diverted from Green Park to Westminster, where it descended beneath the river. From there, the new plans took the railway along the South Bank, through Southwark and Bermondsey, before zigzagging across the river to connect the old dock districts of the Isle of Dogs, North Greenwich and Canning Town. From there the line headed eastwards to Stratford – later to be the centre of a major regeneration programme as the site for the 2012 Olympic Games.

The new Jubilee Line extension opened at the dawn of the new millennium. It represented a new era for the underground railway. Although the trains looked similar to their older counterparts, the new stations were distinctly 21st century. Canary Wharf was emblematic in terms of the new design: gone were the meandering tunnels and glazed tiles, in their place spacious concourses and steel-clad walls. Susan Williams, a photographer from St John's Wood, visited the station shortly after it opened and could barely believe what she saw. 'Instead of finding myself in a series of winding low tunnels like elsewhere on the Tube, I stepped out into a bright and airy station that had an efficient, industrial feel', she recalls. Susan was particularly impressed by the escalator shaft running up to the main entrance. 'It took my breath away. At the top was an enormous glass roof. It was very sunny and the light flooding into the station was incredible. As I stood at the bottom of the escalators and looked up, they were so high that they seemed to be running into the sky.'

London's post-war Tube lines had helped ease congestion on the underground railway, but it was not the only part of the city's 'subterranea' that was struggling to cope with a burgeoning population. Still in east London, the old Blackwall Tunnel was literally crumbling under the weight of traffic that relentlessly passed through. By the mid-1960s, the condition of the tunnel had become so bad that the Greater London Council feared it would have to be closed for essential repairs. Its dilapidated condition was not the only problem. During rush hour, long queues of traffic built up as motorists waited to cross the Thames. A contemporary survey by London Transport showed that motorists had to queue for 10-20 minutes every time they used the tunnel, with the problem worst at the southern entrance. The stream of waiting vehicles had a huge knock-on effect on the surrounding streets, causing stress for local residents who had to contend with the noise and pollution.

The obvious solution to the congestion at Blackwall was to build a second tunnel. Not only would this ease the queues, it would also allow the original tunnel to be closed for much-needed repairs. Thus, in October 1965, contractors Balfour Beatty began work on the £6 million project to build another Blackwall Tunnel.

Initially, construction work made congestion worse as the contractors were forced to close local roads, particularly those near approaches to the tunnel. Harassed residents now not only had to cope with endless queues of traffic, but with dust, mud and the relentless pounding of heavy machinery. Thankfully, progress was swift and, on 3 August 1967, the new tunnel opened. The disruption was far from over, however, as the old tunnel was immediately closed for repairs.

The Blackwall Tunnel project was fully completed in 1969. Once the original tunnel was reopened, traffic travelling north was diverted towards it, leaving the new tunnel to convey motorists southwards.

Although the two tunnels eased traffic congestion in the short term, by the mid-1970s the sheer number of vehicles on the road led to yet more tailbacks at the approaches. Paul Greengrass was nine years old in 1975 and remembers accompanying his van driver father on deliveries during the school holidays. 'The queues at the Blackwall Tunnel were notorious,' he recalls. 'I'll never forget how bored I got sitting in my dad's van as we inched our way through the traffic. All the big lorries had to pull into one lane as the other was too tight for them and this created even more problems, especially when the car drivers wouldn't let them through. The trouble was, there was no other way of getting over to Kent back then. I suppose we could have gone through the Rotherhithe Tunnel or over one of the bridges in central London, but the traffic was bad there too.'

Traffic jams at the Blackwall Tunnel would be a regular sight until 1991, when the QEII Bridge opened on the M25. Although the motorway entailed clocking up many more miles, it became the favoured route across the Thames into Kent for a vast amount of road users.

London's transport network was not the only part of the infrastructure to be feeling the strain. Demands on utilities were also proving to be a challenge. The city's water supply was a particular problem. Many of the old water mains were over 100 years old and in a poor state of repair. Many pipelines lay directly beneath the roads and, as vehicles got heavier, the pressure began to make them crack and rupture. Like the Blackwall Tunnel, London's water pipes were in desperate need of repair but, as they were in constant use, it was almost impossible to achieve. By the 1980s, the situation had degenerated so badly that it was decided a massive, new, deep-level water main had to be constructed, connecting the numerous water treatment works surrounding the capital. This new pipeline would take pressure off the old Victorian pipes and allow damaged sections to be repaired without shutting down the system.

Work on the ambitious new water main began in 1988. Its 'ring of water' ran from Ashford Common in the outer reaches of west London, through Kew and Barnes, before turning northwards and heading under the streets towards Holland Park. From there, it continued in a north-easterly direction before splitting in two. A short spur ran to the New River Head near King's Cross, while the main pipe turned south down Park Lane, crossing the river into Battersea and continuing on its southerly course to Brixton, before turning west and heading through Merton, Raynes Park, Surbiton and Walton. Finally, it crossed the Thames once again before arriving back where it started at Ashford.

The ring main was completed in the late 1990s. Today, the pipe carries around 1,000 million litres of water across the capital every day – about half the total amount consumed. Once the project was finished, a mammoth renovation scheme began on the older mains and plans were drawn up to extend the network even further, creating spurs running from Brixton to the pumping station at Honor Oak in south London, and from King's Cross to Stoke Newington on the north side.

London's water mains were not the only utility requiring constant upgrading. As we have seen, the space directly beneath central London houses a fiendishly complex maze, and its miles of electricity cables also needed constant updating. This made the laying of any additions to the system incredibly complicated.

In 1989, London Electricity was granted permission to construct a substation underneath Leicester Square. However, it needed to be connected with three cable circuits running from an existing substation in Duke Street, Piccadilly, over half a mile away. A feasibility study suggested the new cables would have to be woven through a complex network that stretched deep underground. Near the surface, the new cables would have to avoid hundreds of water pipes, drains and communication cables; if the contractors dug deeper they risked hitting the sewers, and any deep-level tunnelling would have to circumvent no fewer than four Tube tunnels.

It became clear that the new cable route would have to include some sharp twists and turns to avoid interfering with what already lay beneath the streets. In addition, London Electricity was forbidden to dig up the entire route. Instead, Westminster Council insisted a new tunnel be created using hydraulic shields accessed from just four shafts. But how could it be dug without visual awareness of the obstacles it had to avoid?

The task of laying new cables without excavating their route would have been impossible without ground penetrating radar (GPR) – a technology that revolutionised subterranean projects in the late 20th century. This ingenious innovation was first developed in the late 1920s by scientists attempting to gauge the depth of glaciers. However, the full potential of the technology was not explored until after World War 2, as relations between America and the USSR rapidly deteriorated. The US was anxious to set up an airbase within easy striking distance of Moscow, selecting the small town of Dundas on the north-west coast of Greenland. By 1951, the little town had been swallowed up by offices, runways and hangars and the location was renamed Thule Air Base.

Although Thule's location was strategically good, its climate was inhospitable to say the least. Gigantic swaths of ice that covered the coast made landing planes exceptionally tricky, as altitudes were impossible to calculate accurately. After several planes had crashed into the freezing sea, the US Air Force began to investigate the possibilities of ground penetrating radar. The technology allowed pilots to see a detailed picture of the subsurface on which they were landing, as scientists quickly realised it could be used on any terrain. The first commercial GPR system was developed in 1972, since when it has revolutionised tunnelling throughout the world.

CHAPTER 11

ABANDONED UNDERGROUND

Today, London's underground labyrinth is more complex than ever before. Utility pipes and cables snake their way around Bazalgette's monumental sewer system while, further below the streets, Tube trains rattle through the vast network of winding tunnels. Between these main arteries lie the deserted shells of subterranean bunkers and warehouses. In some ways, the city beneath the streets mirrors the city above; some of its structures are old but still useful, while others have been converted for modern requirements. Others still are long-redundant and lie abandoned in the darkness, awaiting resurrection for some new purpose.

One old subterranean structure that has found new life is the Brunels' Thames Tunnel. Its original incarnation as a foot tunnel had ended in 1865, when it was purchased by the East London Railway Company for conversion into a new railway line to serve the busy docks. The old market stalls were swept away amid a flurry of construction work as labourers laid iron tracks along the tunnel floor. Above ground, local residents watched as the old northern entrance shaft was converted into a bright new station named Wapping & Shadwell – the northern terminus for a new railway line.

The East London Railway's new line opened in 1869, running from Wapping, under the Thames to Rotherhithe and then on to New Cross, where it connected with the overground lines of the South Eastern Railway. It proved an instant success and almost as soon as it had opened, plans were drawn up to extend the line further into east London, connecting it directly with the busy London Docks. This new extension tested the skill of the engineers and workmen to the limit, as there was simply no room to take the line above ground and much of the route had to be subterranean. A new terminus (named after the neighbourhood of Shoreditch) was built at Brick Lane, from whence the track ran beneath the goods yard of the Great Eastern Railway before wending its way under Whitechapel to Shadwell, to connect with the Blackwall Railway serving the docks further east. It was here that the engineers faced their greatest challenge, as the new railway had to descend 50ft under the east basin of the London Docks before connecting with the Thames Tunnel at Wapping.

The construction of the tunnel under the dock proved both problematic and costly, not least because it had to be strong enough to support the immense weight of water sitting above it in the dock basin. By 1875, the tunnel under the dock was only half-finished and shareholders were becoming disgruntled at the rising costs and lack of progress. At a tense general meeting in February that year, several shareholders took the directors of the railway to task, as detailed in a subsequent press report. Shareholder Mr Elisart complained that 'the information he had asked for from time to time did not correspond with the facts of the case; the estimates were always exceeded and now (the Railway Company) wanted £400,000 more.' In response, the directors laid blame for the spiralling costs and delays squarely with the London Dock Company, who they claimed had interposed 'technical difficulties' that held up construction to the point that, three years after it had begun, the tunnel under the dock basin remained unfinished.

It was to be several years before the East London Railway was finally completed. The total bill for the works came to a mammoth £3 million, almost double the amount originally projected. Construction costs aside, however, the new line proved to be an important addition to London's railway network, providing a missing link in the chain of communication between the Port of London, the City and beyond.

Although primarily designed to move goods trains about the metropolis, the East London Railway also provided the opportunity for a passenger link between east and west London. In 1884, a spur connecting it with the Metropolitan Railway opened, using St Mary's Station on the Whitechapel Road as its terminus; by 1914, the East London Railway tracks formed part of an Underground passenger service that ran all the way from New Cross to Hammersmith.

Sadly, although the new line looked good on paper, it was never particularly popular with passengers as it lacked interchanges. The service to west London would stop running in the 1940s, while the East London Line reverted to mainly serving goods trains on their way to and from the docks. By the mid-1950s, the profitable continuation of this service was also threatened by road transport, which by now was the dominant form of commercial distribution.

Over the next 25 years, the East London Railway fell into steep decline as the docks it had been built to serve gradually closed. By 1981, the Port of London would cease to exist (with the exception of Tilbury Docks) and it seemed that the Brunels' tunnel would fall into complete disuse. However, in 1987, government-aided redevelopment of the old dock districts gave the line a new lease of life. The Docklands Light Railway opened a station at Shadwell, linking the East London Railway to new developments on the Isle of Dogs. As London's Docklands attracted new business, the railway began to experience a renaissance. By the end of the century it was linked to the West End once again, when an interchange with the Jubilee Line extension was built on the remains of the Surrey Commercial Docks at Canada Water. Today, the former East London Line is part of the London Overground network and runs all the way to West Croydon, with a branch line to Crystal Palace and plans to create a second branch to Clapham Junction.

While the Thames Tunnel found new purpose as a railway, over in north London the old subterranean horse tunnels leading from Euston station to the goods yard at Chalk Farm were put to an altogether unexpected use.

By the early 1960s, the combustion engine had all but wiped out horse-drawn transport, the horse tunnels lying deserted while goods lorries rumbled through the streets above them. One by one, stables at the entrance became vacant as formerly busy tunnels began to fill with builders' materials and general junk. In the early 1980s, it seemed as though the horse tunnels would be lost as architects drew up plans to regenerate the area around Camden Lock by building smart new office and apartment blocks. As the bulldozers and demolition crews moved into the area, there was no one to champion the preservation of the historic tunnels. Indeed, the majority of local residents had no idea that they even existed and the fact that they still stand today is due to a remarkable turn of events.

During the late 1970s, a small market was set up on the banks of the canal next to Camden Lock. At first it made little impact on the area, but, as the years passed, its cheap stalls began to attract young fashion designers and dealers in second-hand clothes. The market steadily grew, developing a reputation for unusual apparel and accessories. As the organisers received more and more enquiries from potential stallholders, the market began to spill over onto the edge of the old railway goods depot. This expansion continued throughout the 1990s and by the turn of the millennium it had spread from its nucleus at Camden Lock, across the old cobbled paths that ran above the horse tunnels and adjacent stables. These former industrial roadways were now filled with colourful stalls selling all manner of goods, from food to fashion. At weekends, the area became a popular meeting place for the young, who browsed stalls or relaxed by the canal before disappearing into Dingwall's dark interior for a lunchtime jazz session.

It was clear by now that the market needed to expand, but the only place to go was underground. The old stables and tunnel entrance (now referred to as 'the catacombs') were opened up to small businesses, quickly filling with stalls selling clothes, jewellery or bric-à-brac, reminiscent of the fairs in the Thames Tunnel 150 years before.

Today, the Camden Horse Market has a unique atmosphere created by its odd juxtaposition of retail outlets and antique stabling. Although the smell of the animals has thankfully long since dissipated, the market is very clearly a stable block – albeit with its horse stalls filled by a diverse array of merchandise rather than hay and livestock.

While the Camden catacombs and Thames Tunnel have found new purpose in 21st-century London, other subterranean sites still languish in decay. In south London, the fire that destroyed the Crystal Palace in 1936 had rendered both the station and the subway that served it virtually redundant. During World War 2, the subway's elegant arches provided temporary shelter for local residents during bombing raids. However, when hostilities ended the site fell back into disuse. Crystal Palace high-level station finally closed in 1954, by which stage the few pedestrians who walked through the empty subway would be hard pressed to imagine how it once echoed with the excited voices of day-trippers.

After the station was demolished in 1961, the subway became a popular retreat for graffiti artists and homeless people searching for shelter. It was eventually bricked up by the local council in the mid-1970s. Today, this last vestige of the extraordinary Crystal Palace is a Grade II listed building, but the only part still visible to the public is the crumbling remains of its once fine entrance on the western side of Crystal Palace Parade, close to the corner of Farquhar Road.

Over in east London, Bishopsgate goods station suffered a similar fate. The depot continued as a busy distribution centre for the national rail network into the 1960s. However, in 1964 disaster struck. At 6am on Saturday 5 December, a safety patrol discovered a fire had broken out on the ground floor of the station. Staff desperately tried to extinguish the flames before they took hold, but a strong wind was blowing on that fateful morning and by the time the fire brigade arrived, the conflagration had spread out of control.

The entire goods depot was evacuated. As workers rushed out of the gates to the safety of the streets beyond, however, they realised to their horror that a section of offices was engulfed in flames, trapping their colleagues inside. Two customs men – 53-year-old George Humphrey and 45-year-old Thomas Tanner – failed to find a way out of the burning building, perishing amid the flames and chokingly acrid smoke.

By the time the fire was brought under control, the grand Victorian building, with its underground warehouse, had been reduced to a smouldering mass of tangled metal girders and smashed glass. Stunned workers stared in disbelief at the wreckage of their workplace. In the days after the fire, the blackened site also became a macabre tourist attraction as Londoners arrived in droves to view its remains.

Following the devastation, Bishopsgate goods station was abandoned. The Great Eastern Railway's goods trains were sent to its satellite depot at Brick Lane or diverted to Liverpool Street, while the remains of the great building were left to slowly decay and the charred remains of its subterranean warehouse became damp, dark and forbidding. Above it, the old platforms were lost under a thick carpet of wild flowers and debris.

Bishopsgate goods station remained in this derelict state for over 30 years. When London Underground unveiled plans to clear the site in 1989, it seemed inevitable that all trace of this once important part of London's commercial life would be erased. Its endurance is the result of an unanticipated discovery.

Back in 1839, when the old Eastern Counties Railway was building its original passenger station at Bishopsgate, the company architect, John Braithwaite, had designed a Gothic-inspired brick viaduct to carry the trains into the terminus. When the station was converted into a goods depot, this viaduct was enclosed by the vaults that formed the underground warehouse and then completely forgotten. However, the proposed demolition of the goods station in 1989 prompted a visit from English Heritage, enquiring as to whether any evidence of the original railway still existed. An investigation of the crumbling basement revealed the remains of Braithwaite's viaduct and a preservation order was quickly issued, citing a 'very early and rare example associated with a first generation London terminus'. English Heritage also saw fit to list the station's main entrance gate and forecourt walls, and it is entirely due to its actions that the remains of Bishopsgate goods station still stand today.

However, while a building of importance was saved from demolition, there was no new use found for it. Today, the once thriving Bishopsgate goods depot stands forlorn at the entrance to Commercial Street, with its gateway boarded up and its buddleia-clad brickwork blackened and crumbling.

While fire had been the nemesis of Bishopsgate goods station, progress destroyed another facet of Victorian underground London. By the beginning of the 20th century, the subterranean pipes of the London Hydraulic Power Company had meandered through the entire metropolis. In the 1930s, when demand was at its peak, the company had over 4,000 customers supplied by six pumping stations at Wapping, Bankside, East India Dock Road, City Road, Rotherhithe and Pimlico. However, following the damage sustained by London factories during World War 2, many companies abandoned the city in favour of new premises out of town. When they left, the demand for hydraulic power went into steep decline. By the late 1970s, the company's last major customer – the docks – had closed. The pumping stations were shut down in 1977 and the network of subterranean pipes sold off to a telecommunications consortium. Today, there is virtually no evidence left above ground of the London Hydraulic Power Company, except for the defunct pumping station at Wapping which has been turned into an arts centre.

By the time that the London Hydraulic Power Company closed its operations, another part of London's underground network was becoming seriously outmoded. In its heyday during the 1960s, the Post Office Railway's driverless trains had carried 40,000 mailbags under London six days a week. Their subterranean stations at Paddington and Liverpool Street linked London's mail distribution system with the rest of the country via the overground railways. In turn, parcels and letters were conveyed across the city to various main post offices, including the huge sorting office at Mount Pleasant. The Post Office was so proud of its unique system that, in 1967, members of the press were invited to take a trip on the railway themselves. *Times* correspondent Philip Howard bravely took them up on the offer:

'The Post Office station, 70ft down, is whitewashed, clean and clinical. Mailbags come hurtling down spiral chutes, on to conveyor belts, into containers, and on to the trains. The man at the automatic train control fiddles knowingly with flashing lights and relay control systems and dead sections of track. "OK Perce, take her away" … Down the 9ft tunnel, along the 2ft gauge, the Post Office train accelerates. Clammy claustrophobia. Near Paddington, the train runs so close to the Metropolitan Line that you can hear Underground travellers talking and doors shutting.'

The Post Office Railway ran 6½ miles across the very centre of London, travelling at 35mph for the eight stations on its route between Whitechapel and Paddington. Following Howard's *Times* report in 1967, it would convey the city's mail for another 30 years. By the new millennium, however, the cost of running the system was beginning to outweigh the obvious benefit of a fast service. The grudging decision was made to shut the railway down and the last train ran on 31 May 2003, since when the tracks have lain idle.

While many mourn the loss of the Post Office Railway, there is less nostalgia for bombing raids. The various shelters and citadels built during World War 2 and the subsequent Cold War now thankfully represent a large proportion of the redundant structures buried under London.

The old Air Ministry citadel at Dollis Hill was taken over by the Post Office when World War 2 ended, used as additional office and storage space for their adjacent laboratory until it relocated in 1976. The original laboratory building and the ground-floor portion of the citadel were briefly used as private offices, but the secret bunker beneath remained empty and gradually filled with water. It stayed in this state until 1997, when the site was sold to a housing association which converted the research buildings into apartments. However, the contract of sale expressly instructed the site's owners to open up the old war bunker to interested members of the public, at least twice a year. Consequently, the water was pumped out and the basement made safe. Today, this little-used relic of the war can be visited every September as part of London's Open House weekend.

Over in Westminster, the Rotundas and the ominously titled 'Steel Frame Building' continued to be used by the government after World War 2, but by the 1960s it was generally felt that the land on which they sat could be put to better use. Plans were drawn up to create a new office complex for the Department of the Environment on the site, incorporating the Rotundas into the new structure. The new development – named Marsham Towers – opened in 1971 and instantly divided public opinion. The scheme comprised three rectangular concrete-and-glass tower blocks that sat on a raised three-storey base. Fans of brutalist architecture admired the building's austerely masculine look. Others simply hated it, branding it ugly and depressing. The architectural critic Nikolaus Pevsner declared Marsham Towers to be 'the very image of faceless bureaucracy' and many people agreed with him.

The controversial development would have a short life. Just 20 years after it had been completed, Secretary of State for the Environment Michael Heseltine announced that he planned to demolish the buildings, without putting forward any suggestions as to what should replace them. The towers remained for another 10 years while ministers deliberated over how best to redevelop the site. The remains of the Rotundas were eventually demolished to make way for Sir Terry Farrell's new Home Office building, which would open in 2002.

While all evidence of the Rotundas' existence has been erased, traces remain of the old war offices at Down Street and Brompton Road Tube stations. Post-World War 2, both sites were decommissioned but the offices remained largely intact. Over the years, the wartime contents of these two fascinating sites gradually disappeared, although some clues as to their unique purpose remain to this day.

At Brompton Road, part of the old Anti-Aircraft Operations Centre has now been taken over by the Ministry of Defence, though the tunnels that lead to their section of the building are bricked up. However, other parts of the station are still accessible to London Underground staff and some of the old wartime offices are still visible along the tunnels. At Down Street, the entire office complex is still accessible. Lines of empty rooms now lie deep beneath Piccadilly, bricked off from passing trains which can be glimpsed through a small emergency exit as they rush through the tunnel. The war rooms were originally left almost totally intact and, had they stayed that way, would have been a unique time capsule preserving a part of London at war. However, over time the offices and corridors were gradually stripped until, today, all that remains is an empty shell.

More wartime relics lie forgotten and disused beneath London's numerous parks and squares. The trench shelters that were dug in these public spaces were grassed over after the war and most are now undetectable, if travelling on foot. However, the foundations of some remain visible from the air. The Greenwich Park trench shelter revealed itself to crane operators helping to build the new wing of the National Maritime Museum, during the dry summer of 2010, when the outline of the shelter's foundations appeared through the scorched grass.

Aerial photographs also reveal the layout of a huge trench shelter in Kennington Park. Chillingly, they also show the spot where the walls of the shelter were blown apart on 15 October 1940, when the trench suffered a direct hit. Over 100 people were killed that night but only 48 bodies were recovered. Thus the shelter became a graveyard. Amazingly, no memorial marked the site of this dreadful tragedy until 2006, when a grey stone tablet was inscribed with the poet Maya Angelou's apt words: 'History, despite its wrenching pain, cannot be unlived, but if faced with courage, need not be lived again.'

Elsewhere in London, many trench shelters have been forgotten as wartime residents died or moved away from the area. Nevertheless, the new millennium has brought renewed interest in some of these forgotten sanctuaries. In 2010, archaeologists unearthed a series of underground shelters at Sunny Hill Park in Hendon. Their work drew a huge amount of interest locally, particularly from young people fascinated to see evidence of how, not so long ago, the area they knew so well was once a place of danger and uncertainty.

Although much evidence of the existence of war bunkers and shelters has long since disappeared, many entrances to the old deep-level Tube shelters remain surprisingly intact and in full view of the public – although most passers-by have no idea of what these rather ugly structures actually were. North of the river, the whitewashed southern entrance to Belsize Park's deep-level shelter stands on the corner of Haverstock Hill and Downside Crescent. A short distance away, the redbrick northern entrance to the shelter at Camden Town can be found on Buck Street, at the junction with Stucley Place. Further into central London, the Goodge Street shelter entrance in Chenies Street is the most recognisable of all deep-level bunkers. Painted cream with red stripes, it stands close to the junction with Tottenham Court Road, its fascia bearing the legend 'Eisenhower Centre' after its most famous occupant.

Over in south London, attempts have been made to make the bland entrance to the Stockwell shelter more interesting by covering it with children's murals, unmistakably visible as one passes by on the South Lambeth Road. The Clapham shelters are harder to spot. The Clapham North shelter stands at the entrance to the Clapham Road Estate, a relic of the war stranded amidst faceless blocks of flats. Close by, the Clapham Common bunker sits derelict and partially hidden behind hoardings at the junction of Clapham High Street and Clapham Park Road. The main entrance to the shelter at Clapham South can be found at the junction of The Avenue and Balham Hill with a second entrance a short distance away, opposite the junction with Gaskarth Road.

Further out of the city, London's Cold War-era Civil Defence Controls were decommissioned at the end of the 1950s, left to crumble away and are largely forgotten. The control centres at Wanstead and Cheam were eventually demolished and the sites redeveloped for housing, but the buildings in Kent and north-west London met an altogether more interesting fate. After being shut down, the Chislehurst centre lay abandoned at the end of a woody track for over three decades, in a progressive state of decay. During this period, plans were put forward to convert it into a recording studio which never got further than the drawing board. The building remained in a derelict state until 1998, when its dilapidated remains were finally saved by a private developer who set about transforming it into a luxury home. Christened 'the Glass House', the resulting building bore little resemblance to the utilitarian structure at its heart. A huge glass roof covered the concrete shell, the interior of which was transformed into an opulent five-bedroom residence with indoor swimming pool and conservatory. Once completed, the developer put it on the market for £3 million.

On the other side of London, the control centre at Partingdale Lane, Mill Hill suffered a similar fate to the Chislehurst site, remaining in a neglected state for 40 years. Nestling in fields down a semi-rural lane, the building was in an attractive location but its only visitors were the local wildlife. However, by the end of the 20th century, demand for housing in London had reached such a level that developers were considering sites that, just a few years previously, they would not have given a second glance. As building frenzy reached fever pitch, the old bunker was finally snapped up by a builder who promptly converted it for residential use. Unlike the Chislehurst property, the bunker's concrete exterior was not softened with an outer shell of bricks (which, in any case, its Grade II listing would not allow). Instead, the outside walls were painted white, accentuating the stark lines even further and harshly contrasting with the countryside that surrounded it. Inside, the bunker was equipped with six bedrooms, luxurious living quarters and a leisure complex, complete with swimming pool and sauna. It was put on the market for £4.5 million in 2010.

Today, the only Civil Defence Control Centre that still exists in its original form is the extraordinary basement of Pear Tree House in Upper Norwood. Despite unwelcome attention from Campaign for Nuclear Disarmament protesters throughout the 1980s, the bunker remained in the use of the London Fire and Civil Defence Authority until 1993. When it moved out, however, alternative tenants could not be found and the centre became a makeshift storeroom while awaiting its next incarnation.

Although remnants of old underground structures and tunnels are scattered about the city, the subterranean spaces that most intrigue Londoners themselves are the disused stations on the underground railway.

CHAPTER 12

GHOST STATIONS

Since its inception nearly 150 years ago, the Tube has become an icon of London. The simple concept of running trains underground revolutionised the city, allowing the metropolis to spread from the agricultural lands of Middlesex to Surrey, while offering its occupants a fast and convenient route back into the city centre.

The underground railway met with instant success and its popularity has endured, despite wartime bombing raids, the rise of the motorcar and terrorism. Even though the city has changed immeasurably since the Metropolitan Railway opened for business, the routes of the Tube are still as relevant today as they were in the Victorian period. However, over time a few stations have been lost. Their demise was usually due to either too much custom (which meant they had to be moved to a more spacious location) or too little (thus rendering a station redundant). Although some of these lost stations were located above ground, many were buried deep beneath the streets. It is these abandoned sections of London's underground labyrinth that are the most intriguing.

Back in 1900, when the Central London Railway opened, the stretch of track between Tottenham Court Road and Chancery Lane was punctuated by a station called 'British Museum'. The station site, at the junction of High Holborn and New Oxford Street, was not particularly close to the museum it was designed to serve and tourists had to work their way north across a series of road junctions before their destination loomed into view. The Central London Railway's directors were seemingly aware of its less-than-perfect location as, by 1914, plans were drawn up to build Central Line platforms at nearby Holborn station. These new platforms would provide a useful interchange with the Piccadilly Line, effectively making British Museum station redundant. However, soon after the plans had been approved, war was declared and all building works on the underground railway came to an abrupt halt. Then, following the war, lack of funds prevented the new platforms being built at Holborn for another 15 years until, in 1933, they were finally completed and British Museum station closed its doors.

Although the station closed in the 1930s, its street-level entrance remained visible for another 60 years, until it was demolished to make way for a new office block in the 1990s. Below the street, the station platforms have long since been removed, but the grimy white-tiled walls of the station can still occasionally be glimpsed from the windows of a passing train.

While the new interchange with the Central Line made Holborn station even busier, another Piccadilly Line station a short distance away did not enjoy the same volume of traffic. At the other end of Kingsway lay Aldwych station – the terminus of a Piccadilly branch line built in 1907 to serve the busy entertainment district on the periphery of the Strand (which was the station's original name). Although the location was good, the infrequency of trains on this little spur of track meant that many theatregoers either walked to their destination from Holborn or got off at Covent Garden, leaving Aldwych station much quieter than intended. The branch closed for the duration of World War 2, but, after hostilities ended, continued to serve Theatreland until 1994, when it finally closed. Today, the two original entrances of the station can still be seen on the Strand and around the corner in Surrey Street, but the platforms beneath lie silent and deserted.

Aldwych was also the site of another abandoned underground station. Aldwych tram station formed the original terminus of a tram line that connected Islington with the West End. The route, which opened in 1906, ran above ground until it arrived at Holborn where it descended into the Kingsway subway, a tunnel that ran beneath the roadway to the terminus at Aldwych.

The tram route initially enjoyed a fair degree of success and, in 1908, the route was extended over the river into south London. However, by the 1920s, it became obvious that the low subway would have to be converted to accommodate double-decker trams if it was to remain an economically viable part of the system. The roadway was lowered in 1929 and trams continued to use the subway throughout the 1930s and 1940s. However, by 1950 the tram network was beginning to be replaced by buses and, in 1952, the Kingsway subway was closed. Following the closure, numerous suggestions were made regarding future use of the tunnel, including proposals to turn it into an underground television studio, a café, a market or even a mushroom nursery. Sadly, none of these innovative ideas ever came to fruition and today the tunnel entrance near Southampton Row looks much the same as it did when the subway first opened. Grey cobbles still cover the roadway, intersected by iron tramlines last used over 50 years ago.

Back on the underground railway, the northern section of the Piccadilly Line harbours another disused and forgotten station. A short distance beyond the great arches of King's Cross station lies the site of two long-abandoned stations, the first of which conveyed north London's dead to their final resting place.

The Great Northern Cemetery in New Southgate was built in the mid-19th century as a solution to north London's overcrowded churchyards, which simply could not accommodate any more bodies. However, although the new cemetery provided plenty of space, it was located several miles from the inner city. Undertakers had traditionally transported the deceased only a short distance and mourners would often walk to the churchyard in which the funeral was being held. This was no longer possible with the new cemetery and so a 'Necropolis Railway' was built, conveying both mourners and deceased to the burial site.

The Great Northern Cemetery station opened in 1861. The accompanying publicity campaign promoted 'Funerals by railway in half the usual time, and at less than half the ordinary cost.' Coffins could be deposited free of charge in the mortuary at the station and customers were offered free railway tickets to visit the cemetery as an added enticement. At first, the service proved popular with London families, but its success was brief. The cemetery at New Southgate was only a 15-minute train ride from King's Cross and many therefore eschewed the cemetery station in favour of more frequent services departing from the main line. Consequently, the Great Northern Cemetery station closed in the late 1860s.

Although the land behind King's Cross no longer accommodated this unusual station, the surrounding area was by no means quiet. On the opposite side of York Road (today's York Way) lay the Great Northern Railway's vast goods depot. The yard was one of the district's biggest employers, particularly in its huge coal warehouses, and residential streets nearby were referred to as the 'Railway Barracks', due to the number of railway employees residing there. On the periphery of the depot, a sizeable potato market also offered steady employment to the residents of the nearby streets.

The busy area caught the attention of the Piccadilly & Brompton Railway which, in 1906, opened a new station to provide passenger transport to and from the depot and market. York Road station sat on land close to the old cemetery station, intended to provide the numerous labourers and porters employed in its vicinity with an easy route to work. However, directors of the railway failed to realise that the majority of the workers they aimed to serve lived within walking distance of their workplace, with therefore little use for the station. Consequently, York Road was underused and, three years after it opened, Sunday services were terminated.

Over the following decades, the coal depot closed down, the potato market relocated to a new site and old residents of the Railway Barracks drifted away from the area. The brick terraces of tiny cottages opposite the coal depot became occupied by some of London's poorest families and gradually deteriorated into slums. As the warehouses and light industry that once surrounded the Great Northern Railway Depot slowly disappeared, the area around York Road station took on an air of desolation. Finally, after years of declining passenger numbers, the station itself finally closed in 1932.

Amazingly, the redundant building survived the slum clearance of the area after World War 2, and by the end of the 20th century the possibility of reopening the station to ease congestion at King's Cross was mooted. When the surrounding land began to be redeveloped as part of the Eurostar project, the old York Road station building was given a facelift in preparation for a resurrection. To date, however, it remains closed, standing incongruously amid a landscape of low prefabricated buildings and grassy wasteland, a relic from the past waiting to find new purpose.

Further east from York Road, the remains of two abandoned City & South London Railway stations lie buried deep beneath the streets. In the heart of the City, next to the Monument, the modern office block Regis House stands on top of King William Street station – the City & South London Line's original north terminus. King William Street opened in the winter of 1890 and immediately became an invaluable part of the City's commuter rail network. However, from the outset, the station's layout and the route of the approach tunnels caused problems. Because it was the last stop on the route, the station had only one track, flanked by two platforms. Passengers disembarked from the train on one platform and boarded on the other, but this system caused severe overcrowding in rush hours and it soon became clear that the layout had to change.

Five years after the station opened, a second track was laid and the platform was moved to an island site in the middle. This helped with the passenger congestion but did not solve another problem. The approach to King William Street station involved a steep climb and sharply curving tunnels, which caused great problems for the trains. The troublesome approach, coupled with the popularity of the line, prompted the directors of the railway to consider extending the line into north London, while simultaneously moving the City station to a more accessible spot. When a potential new site was found in Moorgate, the company quickly put their plans into action. A new tunnel leading from the river to Moorgate was built, bypassing the old route to King William Street. From there, the line continued northwards to a new north London terminus at the Angel in Islington. Works progressed swiftly and, in February 1900, the last train departed from King William Street station.

Surprisingly, the site of the old terminus remained untouched for some years, despite the fact that it was situated on some of the most valuable land in the country. When London Underground finally decided to sell off the property in 1930, they publicised the sale by inviting the press to tour the old station. Visiting journalists found that, to their astonishment, little had changed since the station closed its doors 30 years previously. Although blackened with soot and dust, the pedestrian tunnels and platforms still bore their original tiling and signage, the old wooden signalbox still stood at the end of the platform and, on the walls, dog-eared posters advertised property auctions dating back to 1895.

A private developer eventually purchased the site and, in 1933, the street-level entrance building was demolished. The platform remained intact for some years afterwards but gradually began to lose the fittings and signage that identified it as an Underground station, as visiting workmen surreptitiously took them away as souvenirs or simply threw them in skips. In 1940, the pedestrian tunnels and platform area were converted into an air-raid shelter and what remained of the old 1890s interior was stripped or hidden behind brickwork, where it remains to this day.

The line that replaced the old King William Street route had two interim stations between Moorgate and its terminus at the Angel. Old Street still forms part of the line today, but City Road is almost totally forgotten – although its redbrick ruins can still be seen encasing a ventilation shaft on the corner of Central Street, almost opposite the basin of the Regent's Canal.

City Road station opened in 1901, to serve the light industry that surrounded the busy road from the Angel to Shoreditch. However, like York Road station in King's Cross, it was never well used as most workers in the area lived close to their place of employment. After just two years of service, the company's directors began to discuss City Road's closure and the final blow came in 1913, when the City & South London Railway merged with other lines to form the Underground Group.

The Group wanted to standardise its rolling stock and, to achieve this, the old tunnels from Moorgate to the Angel had to be enlarged. The extension line was closed while the necessary works took place and when it reopened, the station at City Road remained shut.

City Road and York Road are not the only abandoned underground stations in north London. A short distance west lies the still recognisable remains of South Kentish Town station. Built in 1907, it had been part of the Charing Cross, Euston & Hampstead Railway but was never well used, closing in 1924. According to underground legend, shortly after the station ceased operating a train was stopped by signals at the disused platform and an unwitting commuter alighted, only to find himself trapped in the bricked up station. The story caught the imagination of underground staff, one of whom (known only by his initials, 'T.W.') transformed the tale into verse entitled 'The Tale of Mr Brackett' for the staff magazine. The opening stanzas read thus:

> The train to Highgate opened, Mr Brackett stepped without,
> He struck a match to light his pipe – a 'zephyr' blew it out,
> ''Tis strange,' said Mr Brackett, as the train left him behind,
> 'How very dark this station is – good gracious, am I blind?'
> He lit another match and by its feeble little flame,
> He made out 'Benedictine'; then he saw the station name!
> 'Whatever shall I do?' he said, and shouted down the track,
> But no one heard the question and an echo sent it back.
> Then came a distant rumble, and another train swept by,
> Poor Brackett waved and shouted, but it never heard him 'hi',
> And 'til the close of traffic rushing 'Highgates' came and went,
> When Brackett fell asleep against a barrel of cement.

The unfortunate Mr Brackett was eventually rescued after using his last match to light a fire. Sadly, it is not known whether the story has any basis in fact, but it was probably the genesis of a modern urban myth that it is possible to cycle from South Kentish Town to the West End via deserted underground tunnels. Quite where the subterranean cyclists gain access to this dark and treacherous route is a mystery, but it is likely to be near the original frontage of South Kentish Town station, which can still be seen at the junction of Kentish Town Road and Royal College Street.

While the Charing Cross, Euston & Hampstead Railway's station at South Kentish Town had a very brief life, another station on the line was never even completed. Back when the railway was being built, in the early 1900s, the directors originally intended to open a station between the terminus at Golders Green and the stop at Hampstead. A suitable site was found on Hampstead Way, a short distance from its junction with North End Road which, it was decided, would provide the station with its name. The railway company had high hopes for North End station, as it was situated in the middle of land long since earmarked for housing developments. However, in 1904, the influential social reformer and Hampstead resident Henrietta Barnett stopped the builders in their tracks when she arranged for the land opposite the station to be purchased to stop the overdevelopment of Hampstead Heath. No longer with any prospect of the new housing estate ever being built, the railway company shut down the station construction site. The tunnels and platforms were covered over and largely forgotten until after World War 2, when they found an unexpected use.

During the war, London Underground had seen the damage that could be done if bomb-ruptured water pipes started leaking into the railway, realising that if the tunnels under the Thames were hit, the aftermath would be disastrous. As London came under renewed threat during the Cold War, a series of floodgates were installed on the underground railway to minimise damage to the network, should the Thames tunnels be breached. They could be controlled locally by station staff, but it was also considered necessary to create a central control room to oversee the entire system. The unfinished North End station proved the perfect site for the control centre, hidden from view in a location far from the Thames. The necessary equipment was covertly installed and the entrance to the top-secret site disguised as an electricity substation. Although the threat of nuclear war has long since passed, the substation remains, semi-hidden behind a line of fir trees.

Down the hill from Hampstead, in the equally elegant suburb of St John's Wood, lie two more abandoned stations. In 1868, the Metropolitan & St John's Wood Railway opened, providing a link to Swiss Cottage from the busy station at Baker Street. There were two stations in between the termini on this short line, both of which are long disappeared. The first station passengers reached after leaving central London was St John's Wood Road, built primarily to serve the adjacent Lord's cricket ground. During the summer months its platforms were extremely busy, as spectators journeyed to and from the hallowed turf. By the 1920s, the cricket traffic was so heavy that it was deemed necessary to rebuild the station and an attractive two-storey building was constructed, with shops and offices flanking the entrance.

Throughout the roaring 20s, St John's Wood Road station thronged with passengers in the summer months, but its seasonal traffic was to prove its downfall. By the mid-1930s, severe congestion on underground railway tracks in north-west London prompted a new deep-level tunnel to be built between Baker Street and Finchley Road, completely bypassing St John's Wood. Although now it seemed highly likely that the station would be closed, a local campaign to rename it Lord's simultaneously gained momentum. In what now seems like a monumental waste of money, the station's name was officially changed on 11 June 1939, just five months before it closed for good.

The building that housed Lord's station remained on the site for over 20 years following the closure, finally succumbing to redevelopment in the 1960s. The site of the old underground railway station now lies beneath a large hotel on the corner of St John's Wood Road and Wellington Road.

The other intermediate station on the Metropolitan & St John's Wood Railway also fell victim to the new deep-level tunnel. Marlborough Road station stood at the junction of the busy Finchley Road and Queen's Grove, deep in the heart of St John's Wood. Its location in a very affluent, largely residential area where locals could well afford their own private transport meant the little station was never particularly crowded, finally closing its doors on the same day as the neighbouring Lord's station. However, shortly before its closure, Marlborough Road station was the setting for two bizarre accidents which, although seemingly unconnected, occurred in uncannily similar circumstances.

On a cold, wintry day in January 1932, staff at Marlborough Road watched as a train arrived at the northbound platform with the door to one of its carriages swinging open. Inside the empty compartment, a lady's coat, hat and handbag lay neatly on a seat. Concerned, the station workers called for trains to be stopped and ventured into the tunnel, where they soon found a middle-aged woman named Annie Gerrard lying by the tracks in a critically injured state. Miss Gerrard was promptly taken to hospital, but the circumstances surrounding the horrible accident were puzzling. Had she jumped from the carriage intentionally? Had she fallen out of the door, or had she been pushed?

The station staff remained baffled by the accident, but, as time went on, they gradually forgot about the unfortunate Miss Gerrard – until 1937, when it seemed that history was repeating itself. In April of that year, 59-year-old Eva Elsen was found lying seriously injured in the railway tunnel, only a short distance away from the spot where Annie Gerrard had been discovered. The door to the carriage in which she had been travelling was found ajar and her coat was neatly folded on a seat. Mrs Elsen was taken to hospital but, sadly, succumbed to her injuries before she could be interviewed by the police. Whether the two accidents were in some way connected, or were merely a very unhappy coincidence, was never discovered. It also remains unknown as to whether or not the two women jumped out of the carriage intentionally.

Two years after Eva Elsen's accident, Marlborough Road station closed and its platforms were demolished. The street-level building remains and, for many years, the ticket office found an unlikely use as a Chinese restaurant.

Although some Underground stations have ceased to exist completely, others have simply moved location and the remains of their original sites have disappeared into the dark, winding tunnels of the network. These abandoned stations tend to stay in a permanently redundant state, but one enjoyed an unexpected reincarnation many years after it closed.

Tower of London station was opened in 1882 by the Metropolitan Railway on the east side of Trinity Square. The entrance building was constructed in remarkably quick time, taking just two days and three nights to complete and the station's lifespan proved equally short. Just two years after it opened, the Inner Circle Line's Mark Lane station was completed on nearby Byward Street, almost opposite All Hallows Church. With no need for two stations in such close proximity to each other, the Metropolitan Railway closed Tower of London just one week after Mark Lane opened. But this was not the end for the redundant site.

Mark Lane station was renamed Tower Hill in 1946. By this time, the station was extremely busy and desperately needed to enlarge its facilities, but there was no room to expand at the Byward Street site and so new locations were sought to which the station could be relocated. Ironically, the old Tower of London station proved the best bet. Building works commenced on new platforms and a ticket hall and, in 1967, the new Tower Hill station opened to the public. The old site at Byward Street was shut down and all that remains of it today is a subway under the busy road.

Not far from Tower Hill, the station at Aldgate East on the edge of the City was also moved. The original station opened in October 1884, near the corner of Whitechapel High Street and Goulston Street, as a single-storey L-shaped building sandwiched between much taller retail premises and Edward Toplis's tobacco manufactory. Its main entrance was on Whitechapel High Street, while the side exit took passengers out to where Tubby Isaac's famous seafood stall now stands, outside the Aldgate Exchange pub.

Shortly before World War 1, the building was reconstructed and a second floor added, making the frontage considerably more imposing and also providing a large smoking room for patrons. However, this new station was destined to have a short life. After the war, the need for longer trains on the busy District Railway prompted the station's move to a larger new site on the corner of Whitechapel High Street and Commercial Street where it remains to this day, the old station closing on 31 October 1938. Although its smart stone façade is long since demolished, pillars of the old platforms can still be spied from westbound trains as they leave the current station.

Aldgate East's relocation signalled the end for another Underground station further down the line. St Mary's station, which once formed part of the Metropolitan Railway's early attempt at an east/west cross-route, occupied a site on the south side of the Whitechapel Road, close to where the East London Mosque now stands. It closed just as the new Aldgate East station opened in 1938, but quickly found use as an air-raid shelter. The platforms were bricked off from the railway line and lined with rows of crudely constructed benches, which were occupied almost nightly during the Blitz. Although the platforms are no longer entirely visible because of the separating wall, their edges can still be seen from passing trains, along with the tops of the original cast-iron pillars supporting the station's barrel-vaulted ceiling.

The remains of another relocated station can be glimpsed from passing trains at Stockwell. The original Stockwell station was opened as the southern terminus of the City & South London Railway in 1890. The building was a pleasing brick-built affair with a curved entrance lobby and a handsome domed roof, which concealed the machinery for two lifts to take passengers down to the island platform. The success of this innovative line, which carried commuters under the Thames into the City, ensured Stockwell did not remain a terminus for long. By 1900, the line had been extended to Clapham Common and, in 1923, the station underwent a major renovation. The old building was replaced by a decidedly less attractive art deco entrance, but access to the platform was improved considerably by the installation of escalators. The street-level section of Stockwell station was not the only part of the site to be transformed. Below ground, the old island platform was abandoned and two new platforms were constructed, this time in separate tunnels. Today, the 1920s entrance has been replaced with an even uglier building. Beneath it, however, the twin-tunnel platforms are still in use and trains still pass through the site of the original platform, situated just north of the current site.

Although Stockwell's platforms were moved, the rest of the station stayed put. This was not the case for two other Underground stations further west. The Bakerloo Line's deep-level tunnel from Baker Street not only spelled the end for Lord's and Marlborough Road stations, but also prompted relocation of the original terminus of the Metropolitan & St John's Wood Railway at Swiss Cottage.

The original Swiss Cottage station lay on the opposite side of the Finchley Road to today's main entrance. The ground-level booking hall stood at the corner of Belsize Road (before its exit onto the Finchley Road was plugged by an office development). In the 1920s, the entrance was substantially redeveloped and incorporated into a pleasant shopping arcade faced with white faience tiles. The layout of Swiss Cottage station reflected a time when travel – even on the Tube – was far more glamorous than it is today. Passengers could dine in the street-level buffet before descending the stairs to the platforms; one can imagine fashionable ladies chatting excitedly over a light lunch before embarking on a West End shopping trip. However, World War 2 put a stop to such refined activities, with both the buffet and ticket office closing in 1940. Today, the entire shopping arcade has been replaced and the original entrance to Swiss Cottage station is merely a faceless underpass to the modern platforms.

Further west, the original underground station at Earl's Court met a similar fate. The first station to serve this area of London was built by the Metropolitan Railway opposite today's entrance on Earl's Court Road. At the time of its construction the area had more market gardens than people, its underground station comprising just a small wooden building at street level, with staircases at the rear that led down to the platforms. During the 1870s, the Metropolitan District Railway built a line extension to West Kensington and Hammersmith. Shortly after it had been completed, the little ticket office at Earl's Court burned to the ground, although the fire, in which no one was injured, proved something of a godsend for the railway. The original station's proximity to the junction of the new District Railway had resulted in a good deal of congestion on the surrounding tracks, and so, when the original station was destroyed, the decision was made to move it across the road to its present site.

The relocation of Earl's Court station proved timely. During the 1890s, the scrubland that lay behind the new station by the side of Warwick Road was adopted as a showground. Londoners flocked there to see Buffalo Bill's Wild West Show and to ride on a huge observation wheel that had been erected. The shows and fairs continued to be popular into the 20th century and, in 1935, Earl's Court Exhibition Centre was built on the site. Opening for business on 1 September 1937, the venue first hosted a 'Chocolate & Confectionery Exhibition' and was an instant success. Events held there in the following years attracted so many visitors that Earl's Court station was enlarged to incorporate a second street-level exit on Warwick Road and an underground foot tunnel leading from the station's Piccadilly Line platforms, beneath the road and straight into the exhibition centre's foyer.

Earl's Court Exhibition Centre has been a London landmark for over 70 years. However, plans are now afoot to redevelop the site and convert the venue into luxury housing. If this goes ahead, the drop in passenger numbers at Earl's Court station may well result in part of it disappearing into the fascinating world of London Underground's abandoned stations.

CHAPTER 13

TRACKING LONDON'S LOST RIVERS

More obscure than even the best hidden of London's abandoned Tube stations are the city's lost rivers. These ancient waterways have long since been encased in pipes and hidden from view, but it is still possible to find clues to where they once coursed from their rural sources, down the hills into the Thames Valley.

The waters that form the Fleet River rise at Hampstead, appearing above ground at Hampstead Ponds and then at several wells along its course. In addition to being remarkable relics of a time before piped water, these wells provide excellent markers to track the route of the underground river.

Close to the Fleet's source is the Chalybeate Well in Well Walk – an elegant avenue leading to Hampstead Heath's perimeter. This natural well, which was discovered in the mid-1600s, yielded water with a high iron content known as chalybeate water. At the time of its discovery it was considered to be excellent for delicate constitutions, and by the early 1700s the well had become quite a landmark. An impressive ballroom and pump room were built close by to cash in on the crowds that it drew.

Chalybeate water continued to be a popular medicine throughout the 1700s, particularly for ailments of the nervous system. By the end of the century, one Dr Austin made a small fortune from his Chalybeate Pills, which apparently possessed the essential elements of the efficacious waters. Dr Austin targeted his marketing at women, claiming that his pills could cure 'young females [of] all Hysterical Affections, Nervous Head-aches, etc.', while also helping mothers 'debilitated by bad lyings-in, by too-long suckling, or by frequent miscarriages'. Boxes of his pills could be purchased at Francis Newberry's warehouse at St Paul's Churchyard for 3s 6d plus 6d tax.

It is not known whether Dr Austin's Chalybeate Pills had an impact on the popularity of Hampstead's well, but, by the turn of the century, the crowds that once frequented the pump house were thinning. As medicinal waters were forced to compete with more scientifically proven remedies and local residents signed up to have water piped direct to their homes, the well fell into disuse and silted up. By the 1870s, both the well and Well Walk itself faced demolition for the building of a new housing estate.

However, the area's rich heritage saved both from destruction and served to benefit the well. As part of the revised development layout, the ground around it was bored and new springs were found. These were diverted into the well, which at the time was in a sorry state of repair. With its waters now revived, plans were laid to restore the well-head, the results of which can be seen today a short distance down Well Walk, as it leads from the heath.

Further into London, the course of the River Fleet is marked by several other wells, most notably the 'Clerk's Well' which gave Clerkenwell its name. The area had been noted for its wells long before the Fleet disappeared from view. Indeed, in the late 1100s, the historian FitzStephen noted that 'round London, on the northern side… [there are] excellent springs, the water of which is sweet, clear and salubrious, amongst which Holywell, Clerkenwell and St Clement's Well are of most note and most frequently visited, as well by the scholars from the schools, as by the youth of the city, when they go out to take air in the summer evenings'. The Clerk's Well was closed off in the 1850s, but its remains were excavated during the construction of Well Court on Farringdon Lane and the old well-head can now be spied through one of the ground-floor windows.

Another famous site supplied with water from the Fleet was Bagnigge Wells. This ancient well is identified by a plaque featuring a man's head set into the wall of numbers 63 and 65 Kings Cross Road. Like the Chalybeate Well at Hampstead, the two springs that formed Bagnigge Wells became a popular spa in the 18th century, where the fashionable of London came to socialise and take the waters. According to legend, the wells got their name from Bagnigge House which once stood on the site, a smart property tenanted by Nell Gwynne, the mistress of Charles II. At the time when Miss Gwynne lived there, the Fleet still ran above ground through the grounds of the house itself.

Hampstead is the location of another subterranean river. Although buried underground today, the waters of the Westbourne once filled Branch Hill Pond, which stood on Branch Hill near West Heath Road. The pond survived until the 19th century and was immortalised by the artist John Constable in the 1820s. His romantic rendition of the pond depicts the surrounding area as ruggedly rural; livestock graze near the water's edge as the Westbourne cascades from a conduit. Today, the pond is long gone but the slope of Branch Hill still becomes waterlogged during very wet weather, giving a tantalising glimpse of the source that once existed there.

From Hampstead, the Westbourne flows unseen down the hill, crossing today's Finchley Road at the junction of Cannon Hill. There is a slight undulation of the road here, showing where the river once flowed. From there, it used to run through the old village of West End before descending towards the metropolis. On its journey to the Thames, the Westbourne passed through Kilburn, where wells fed by the river were once a feature of the area. Amazingly, one survived the intense suburban development of the area in the late 19th and early 20th centuries, its head still seen in the grounds of a rather uninspiring council estate at the back of Kilburn Park Tube station.

From Kilburn, the Westbourne's subterranean route takes it down Kilburn Park Road and Shirland Road, through the elegant avenues of Maida Vale, to Bayswater. Little overground evidence of the river can be found here, although the 17th-century Swan Inn on the Bayswater Road hints that the hostelry once stood close to the riverbank.

The Westbourne then travels under Hyde Park, where its waters once fed the Serpentine until they became too polluted, into Knightsbridge, site of a long-lost river crossing. At the bottom of Sloane Street, the river makes a surprising appearance at Sloane Square Underground station, where a metal pipe carries it over the railway tracks. It then flows down past the Royal Hospital before being disgorged into the Thames at Chelsea Embankment. It is here that the Westbourne is at its most visible, as the arched opening reaches halfway up the embankment wall and, at low tide, the river waters can be seen flowing across the mudflats of the Thames.

Like the Fleet and the Westbourne, the waters of the Tyburn River also formed wells, all sadly now lost under centuries of building works. One of its most famous wells was situated on the east side of Shepherd's Fields – a belt of arable land running between Hampstead and the village of West End, close to the northern end of today's West End Lane. The 'Shepherd's Well', as it was known, was said to have waters so pure that they never froze, even in the coldest weather. The well provided the local residents with drinking water for centuries, but when the New River Company began to offer domestic water supplies, it gradually fell out of use. The smart railings and arch that had once surrounded it became dilapidated, and by the 1870s the well was described by writer Edward Walford as a 'muddy swamp'. Soon after it was lost forever, as the Shepherd's Fields disappeared under new housing developments, but it is believed that the site of the well was somewhere close to the junction of Church Row and Fitzjohn's Avenue.

From Hampstead, the Tyburn flows down the slopes of the hill into central London. Today, its first appearance above ground is concealed from view inside the Charlbert Bridge (opposite the end of Charlbert Street, London NW8), which was constructed to convey both pedestrians and the Tyburn across the Regent's Canal into Regent's Park.

The Tyburn waters make their second above-ground appearance at the park's boating lake but soon descend beneath the streets again, undetectable until they reach Marble Arch. This busy part of the West End was once the junction of Tyburn Road (now Oxford Street) and Tyburn Lane (now Park Lane) and the site of the notorious 'Tyburn Tree', a three-legged gibbet on which the capital's most notorious criminals met their fate. Today, nothing is left of the gruesome gallows, but a little-seen plaque set into a traffic island marks where it once stood and a memorial on the nearby Tyburn convent commemorates 105 Catholic martyrs hanged there between 1535 and 1681.

The Tyburn next appears in a most unlikely place – the basement of Gray's Mews Antiques Market, just off Oxford Street. When the market's founder, Bennie Gray, moved into the premises in the 1970s, he found the basement was submerged under water. On further investigation, it became clear that the water originated from the Tyburn river. Rather than cover it over, Gray decided to make it a feature and, today, visitors to the market can see the river flowing through the basement, complete with a stock of fish. After briefly revealing itself at Gray's Mews, the Tyburn then descends back under the streets and wends its way to the Thames, completely obscured from view.

Further west, all that remains above ground of Counter's Creek is a soggy ditch beside Platform 4 of West Brompton station. From there, the tracks of the London Overground line mirror the course of the river as it flows underground past Brompton Cemetery and Chelsea Football Club. The club's stadium – Stamford Bridge – is named after a river crossing that once straddled Counter's Creek at the Fulham Road. The railway then continues to follow the route of the creek past the new Imperial Wharf station and into the Thames at Sands End.

Over in the City, the Walbrook has completely vanished from view. Long ago, the river was an important feature of the metropolis. The Romans used it both for transporting goods into the city and as a sacred place of worship, building a temple to Mithras on its banks. The temple was rediscovered in 1954, when the area was redeveloped, and, for a while, provided a good indicator of where the Walbrook lay beneath the streets. However, development of this prime piece of real estate meant that the temple could not remain in its original position for long, its move to a less obstructive location negating its function as a marker for the Walbrook.

Today, the ancient river survives above ground in name only. The Ward of Walbrook is one of the modern City's smallest wards, but nevertheless contains some important buildings within its boundaries such as the Bank of England, the Mansion House and the ancient church of St Stephen Walbrook. On the banks of the Thames, Walbrook Wharf marks the spot where the river once flowed out into the Thames.

Although the Walbrook has long since been obscured from view, some Londoners feel there is a strong case for liberating its waters from their underground pipes and bringing it to the surface once again. Plans have been drawn up to describe ways in which the river could become a natural focal point of this densely developed part of the City. The concept is undoubtedly interesting, but, unfortunately, the sheer number of roads and buildings that would have to be demolished or radically altered to accommodate the waterway renders it virtually impossible to realise. For the foreseeable future at least, the Walbrook is destined to stay beneath the streets.

Over in south London, the city's underground rivers are frustratingly difficult to track at street level. Clues to the route of the Falcon can be found at the eponymous road near Clapham Junction (which flooded in 2007 when the brook burst out of its confines during heavy rain) and the Falcons Estate. The Effra, which once flowed through the rural fields of Dulwich and Brixton, now courses silently through Bazalgette's sewer system. The river has two branches: the first rises at Crystal Palace and flows under West Norwood to the South Circular Road; the other rises at Gipsy Hill and travels under Clive Road and then Croxted Road, where it meets the Crystal Palace branch. It then continues under Croxted Road to Herne Hill station and along the perimeter of Brockwell Park to its namesake, Effra Road. From there it travels northwards under Brixton Road, turning west near The Oval before emptying into the Thames near Vauxhall Bridge.

A little further east, the Earl's Sluice and its sister river, the Peck, display virtually no evidence of their existence above ground once they reach inner London. The only clues are place names and even these are obscure. Camberwell, through which the waters of the Earl's Sluice once flowed, suggests the presence of wells at some point in its history. As long ago as 1796, before the land had been completely built over, the antiquary Daniel Lysons searched for clues to why Camberwell was thus named, but was forced to admit, 'I can find nothing satisfactory with respect to its etymology; the termination seems to point out some remarkable spring.' The parish church of Camberwell is dedicated to St Giles – the patron saint of outcasts – and some historians have suggested that the area may have been a place to which the afflicted came in search of a cure, perhaps to be found in the waters of a well. It is known that the area did possess several wells, though their location is unknown today, as is whether any of them supposedly produced miraculous waters.

Near Bermondsey, the mysterious Earl's Sluice is joined by the Peck – the river that gives its name to Peckham. The Peck flows above ground from Honor Oak in south London and disappears only when it reaches Peckham Rye. The combined waters of the two rivers then travel beneath the streets, briefly appearing above ground to cross a railway line at Surrey Quays before descending once again to the old Surrey Commercial Docks – where they flow out into the River Thames.

CHAPTER 14

INTO TOMORROW

Despite the fact that some elements of London's underground labyrinth now lie disused and forgotten, the vast majority of this subterranean network of pipes, tunnels and cables is still very much part of the city's infrastructure.

Although essentially a Victorian concept, the Tube continues to be the fastest route around the capital – although, in summer, the older deep-level tunnels can be unbearably hot and claustrophobic. During the stifling heatwave of 2006, it was rumoured that temperatures hit 47° on the Central Line, while travellers on the other deep-level lines fared little better. Commuters found the stifling temperatures horribly uncomfortable, but, discouragingly, there seemed to be little that they or London Underground could do about it.

When the first underground railway lines were built, the metropolis was considerably less extensive both above and below ground. As new tunnels and pipes were introduced and new buildings covered the terrain above, the heat they produced spread deep under the ground. As a consequence, the tunnels of the underground railway are now up to 30° warmer than they were when they first became operational.

Solutions to the problem have been sought for over 70 years, but to date, no resolution has been found. However, while it seems that the Tube will remain hellishly hot in summer, plans are afoot to at least improve congestion, particularly during the dreaded rush hour.

In 2008, royal assent was given for a new underground railway through the centre of London. This new line will form part of the Crossrail service, connecting Maidenhead and Heathrow in the west with Shenfield and Abbey Wood in the east, using overground-size trains capable of holding 1,500 passengers.

The new line will travel above ground until it reaches the approach to Paddington, from whence it will disappear into new twin tunnels. Its first subterranean stop will be at a new Paddington station, located underneath Eastbourne Terrace and Departures Road, to be accessed by street-level escalators. From there, the track will travel direct to the heart of the West End, stopping at another new station at Bond Street with two entrance halls: one at Davies Street and the other on Hanover Square. A new subterranean foot tunnel will connect it with the existing Bond Street station.

The new station at Bond Street will cross the banks of the ancient Tyburn River. Prior to work on the new station buildings commencing, a team of archaeologists were invited to survey the site and their findings were intriguing. Their dig uncovered numerous clay pipes, pottery and bricks dating back to the early 1600s – a time when it was previously thought that this part of the West End comprised only fields and a few farm buildings. It seems that the Crossrail project may have inadvertently unearthed a hidden part of London's history.

From Bond Street, the new line will travel to Tottenham Court Road station, which will be completely redeveloped with a new entrance on Dean Street. From there it will travel into the City via Farringdon. Two new platform tunnels will be built here, connecting two new ticket halls. A foot tunnel will also connect Farringdon with Barbican station, an approximate five-minute walk away.

The next station on the line will be Liverpool Street, which will have tunnels linking to Moorgate. From there, the railway will travel under the city to Whitechapel, where a brand-new entrance hall will be built at Durward Street, providing alternative access to the station. The existing main entrance will remain in its original position and a glass-covered walkway will connect the two.

The Crossrail's final stop before re-emerging above ground will be Canary Wharf. The entrance to this station will sit in the centre of the old North Basin of the West India Docks, surrounded by water and accessed by bridges.

It is hoped by developers and commuters alike that the Crossrail line will reduce overcrowding on other underground lines. The projections certainly appear promising. When completed, the new railway will run 24 trains each way per hour during the busiest times, with the journey from Liverpool Street to Bond Street estimated at just seven minutes.

The underground railway is not the only part of London's subterranean labyrinth to expand. In east London, work is underway to build a new four-mile tunnel under the River Lea from Stratford to Beckton. This tunnel, which is being constructed by Thames Water, will convey sewage to the treatment works at Beckton which, at present, intermittently overflows into the river.

However, while the intention is to make the Lea a much cleaner, safer waterway, the Thames is gradually becoming more polluted.

The post-war expansion of London has brought unprecedented pressure on the capital's entire sewer system. Although Bazalgette's intercepting sewers are still amazingly efficient, they are gradually getting fuller. While this presents no problem during dry weather, heavy rainfall causes the overloaded sewers to overflow directly into the Thames. In total, nearly 40 million cubic metres of untreated sewage currently finds its way into the Thames each year. In some spots, sewage escapes on an almost weekly basis, after just 2mm of rainfall.

Although it is thankfully unlikely that the Thames will return to the dreadful state it was in at the time of the Great Stink, there are strong environmental reasons to get rid of the untreated sewage currently invading the river. In order to do this, Thames Water has put forward a proposal to build a massive tunnel under the Thames to convey any overflow directly to the Beckton treatment works.

This new 'Thames tunnel' would measure an enormous 23ft in diameter and run 250ft beneath the city for 14 miles. The suggested route would take it from storm tanks in Acton down to Hammersmith pumping station. From there, it would shadow the route of the Thames to Limehouse and then turn north-east, travelling under the Limehouse Cut to Abbey Mills pumping station, where it would connect with the new Lea tunnel.

The Thames tunnel is currently at the consultation stage and the project is liable to be fraught with controversy. The works would cause a huge amount of disruption through the most built-up areas of the city and the £3.6 billion construction costs would be met by Thames Water's customers, whose water bills would rise considerably. Whether the disruption and spiralling tariff are worthwhile, set against the environmental cost if the Thames continues to have raw sewage pumped into it, is a moot point.

Many Londoners will no doubt balk at the astronomical cost of a sewage tunnel. For them, the subterranean city could be used for more practical purposes, such as underground car parks and roadways to ease the chronic traffic congestion that has blighted the city for many decades. As the capabilities in tunnel engineering advance, there is little doubt that the land under London will form a crucial part of schemes that are currently deemed impossible.

Perhaps the most tantalising of these is the creation of a transatlantic tunnel linking Europe to America. The idea of a subaqueous tunnel under the Atlantic Ocean is not new. Back in 1895, *The Strand Magazine* published a story by Michel Verne (son of Jules) in which a tunnel linking Boston to Liverpool was created. Since then, many have tried to originate a scheme that turns the dream into a reality – but none have progressed further than the conceptual stage. One imaginative proposal from the 1960s eschewed Boston and Liverpool in favour of termini at New York and London. Trains suspended by magnetic levitation were propelled along a vacuum tunnel at speeds of up to 5,000mph, thus cutting the journey time between the two continents to just under one hour.

Although the concept is hugely inspiring, in reality a transatlantic tunnel would be fraught with unknowns. After all, what would happen if a train broke down or there was a fire onboard? The passengers could hardly walk along the track to the nearest exit. Ultimately, at present, the monumental amount of money and research such a project would require makes it extremely unlikely for the foreseeable future.

Far more likely is the prospect that underground London will continue to be used in the same way as it always has – to convey people and utilities around the city and, in times of conflict, to provide shelter. Ever since London's rivers were driven underground and used for carrying away the city's waste, the subterranean city has been an essential but often overlooked part of London's infrastructure. As we walk the city's streets, this vast underground labyrinth continues to lie hidden beneath our feet.

POSTSCRIPT

TYBURN RIVER WALK

Introduction

London's lost rivers form a mystical part of the city's underground labyrinth. For centuries, these ancient waterways have lain largely forgotten under the bustling thoroughfares, confined in pipes but still flowing silently beneath our feet.

This walk traces the subterranean route of the River Tyburn, once famed for its clear waters that never froze even in the depths of winter. Once a vital source of water for Londoners, the Tyburn has almost completely vanished from view. As we follow its course from the hills of Hampstead to the great River Thames, however, we can imagine how the surrounding landscape might have looked when the river flowed above ground, coursing its way down the slopes of the Thames Valley before splitting in two at Westminster to form Thorney Island, on which Edward the Confessor built his majestic abbey.

Long ago, the Tyburn was known as Teo Burns – two brooks – and, as the name suggests, the river has two sources, both at Hampstead, buried deep beneath the 19th-century housing estates west of Rosslyn Hill. The eastern source flows down Belsize Avenue before entering St John's Wood, where it meets the western source – the branch that we are about to track.

This walk is divided into two parts. However, if you are feeling energetic it is possible to walk the whole route in around three hours.

Part 1 – Hampstead to Regent's Park

Start: Hampstead Tube station
Finish: Regent's Park garden café
Time: Approximately 1hr 20min
Notes: There are shops, pubs and cafés along the route at Hampstead, Swiss Cottage and Charlbert Street. Public toilets can be found at the boating lake in Regent's Park.

From Hampstead station, cross over the High Street and walk south down Heath Street, which becomes Fitzjohn's Avenue.
At the junction of Fitzjohn's Avenue and Lyndhurst Road, you will see a plaque marking the site of the Shepherd's Well, where once the waters of the Tyburn formed a spring close to the river's source. Until the 19th century, Hampstead was separated from London by a broad swath of meadows known as Shepherd's or Conduit Fields. The Shepherd's Well once lay on the eastern edge of the fields and was renowned for its crystal-clear water.

Continue down Fitzjohn's Avenue towards Swiss Cottage.
The Tyburn is flowing underground beneath your feet on the left-hand side of the road.

Continue south into College Crescent.
At the junction of College Crescent and Fitzjohn's Avenue, you will see an octagonal gazebo on your right. This rather picturesque structure houses the Palmer Drinking Fountain, presented to the Borough of Hampstead in 1904 by the family of the late Samuel Palmer, as a memorial to the co-founder of Huntley & Palmer biscuits. Palmer lived close to the site of the fountain, at 40 College Crescent.

Carry on down College Crescent towards the junction with the busy Finchley Road. Here, College Crescent becomes Avenue Road. Continue south down this road, past Swiss Cottage Tube station, until you come to a busy crossroads with Swiss Cottage library on the corner.
The area's unusual name is derived from the pub that stands in the centre of this rather noisy intersection. The current Swiss Cottage replaced the earlier Swiss Tavern, built next to an old tollgate leading into London in 1803/4.

Continue over at the crossroads and keep following Avenue Road.
This road contains some of London's most expensive real estate, with properties often changing hands for well over £10 million. Some of the houses are now embassies but the majority are still private homes.

Continue along Avenue Road until you reach Queen's Grove on your right. Turn right into Queen's Grove, then first left into Woronzow Road.
This is where the eastern and western sources of the Tyburn join together before flowing into central London.

Woronzow Road is named after Count Simon Woronzow, who came to London as the Russian ambassador in 1789. Woronzow lived in Marylebone and, when he died in 1832, left a financial bequest to the poor of the parish. The money was used to build the Marylebone Almshouses on St John's Wood Terrace, which is on the next stage of our route.

Continue down Woronzow Road (across the junctions of Norfolk Road and Acacia Road) to the junction with St John's Wood Terrace.
On the corner of these two streets are the Marylebone Almshouses. Sadly, the houses built using Count Woronzow's bequest have long since disappeared. The estate we see today was built in 1965, on the footprint of the original.

Continue right into St John's Wood Terrace until you reach The Star pub, then turn left into Charlbert Street, across the junction with Allitsen Road.
Here we find another Victorian drinking fountain, with a religious inscription carved into the granite. A little further down Charlbert Street, at numbers 42-48, is the RAK recording studio, created out of an old school and church hall in 1976 by record producer Mickie Most. In many ways a predecessor to Simon Cowell, Most worked with some of the most commercially successful pop acts of the 1970s and was a judge on TV talent show *New Faces*. In the close of the decade he produced the more credible music show *Revolver*, giving exposure to artists such as The Jam (whose nightmarish song 'Down in the Tube Station at Midnight' followed soon after).

Carry on down Charlbert Street to the junction with Prince Albert Road. Cross over Prince Albert Road onto the Charlbert footbridge, leading into the park.
The Tyburn crosses the Grand Union Canal here, in a pipe concealed under the bridge.

Once over the bridge, continue straight onto the Outer Circle.
On your right, the ornate wrought-iron gates guarded by armed police mark the entrance to Winfield House, home of the US ambassador. The Tyburn flows under the grounds of this palatial property, which necessitates a short detour.

Cross over the Outer Circle and take the footpath straight ahead into Regent's Park. Where the path splits, take the right-hand fork. After a short distance, the path splits again. Take the right-hand fork down to the boating lake.
Masking the original course of the Tyburn, this lake was created by the great architect John Nash, who began laying out Regent's Park in 1818. Originally part of an unfulfilled scheme to build a grand palace for the Prince Regent, the park was not opened to the general public until 1835. Since then, it has served as a much-needed open space for Londoners.

Turn left and follow the path around the perimeter of the lake until you arrive at a bridge on your right. Cross over the bridge and continue down the footpath until you reach the Inner Circle.

Turn right at the Inner Circle. Soon you will see the Garden Café on your left. Stop here for some well-earned refreshment!
Part one of the Tyburn River Walk finishes here. The following instructions will take you to Baker Street, where you can either continue on the second part of the walk or catch a train from Baker Street Tube station.

Once out of the café, take the signposted footpath to Clarence Gate. Follow the path around, past the bandstand, then cross the bridge on your right over the lake. Once over the bridge, turn right and take the first path left out of the park. Cross the road, turn right and follow it round out of Clarence Gate. Baker Street is straight ahead of you.

Walk down Baker Street, past the Sherlock Holmes Museum on your right, until you get to Baker Street Underground station (Hammersmith & City, Metropolitan, Circle, Bakerloo and Jubilee Lines).

TYBURN RIVER WALK Part 2 – Gloucester Place to the Thames

Start: Baker Street station
Finish: Houses of Parliament, Westminster
Time: Approximately 1hr 30min
Notes: Allow more time if you want to browse Gray's Antiques Market (open Monday-Saturday) or visit the Guards' Museum (open daily, 10-4). There are plenty of pubs and cafés along the route.

On exiting Baker Street station, turn right onto Marylebone Road.
Opened in 1863, Baker Street station was one of the original stops on the Metropolitan Railway – the world's first underground line.

Cross over Baker Street to take the first turning on the left into Gloucester Place.
The Tyburn flows directly under this busy street after emerging from Regent's Park.

Continue along Gloucester Place for some distance.
This fine old street of attractive Georgian houses has been home to several London luminaries over the years. The portrait painter Sir Gerald Kelly lived at number 117 from 1916 until his death in 1972. The photographer Tony Ray-Jones had a studio and flat at 102. Number 48 was the home of John Robert Godley, Irish statesman and founder of Canterbury, New Zealand, while number 65 was the home of the great Victorian writer William 'Wilkie' Collins. Many of these elegant houses are now hotels or embassies.

Turn left into Blandford Street.
We are now turning eastwards, following the Tyburn on its way to the West End.

Carry on down Blandford Street, across Baker Street and Manchester Street, until the junction with Marylebone High Street.
The name Marylebone derives from its medieval name, Maryburne, meaning 'St Mary's brook'. Before the 1400s, the area was known as Tiburne (first recorded under this spelling in 1086) and Teyborne (1312), after the river that ran through it.

Cross over the High Street into Marylebone Lane.
The Angel in the Fields pub on the corner recalls a time long ago when the lane was surrounded by countryside. Any remnants of Marylebone Lane's rural past have long since disappeared, but some of the businesses along this little street have been around for some time. One of the oldest, the Golden Hind fish and chip shop at number 73, was established in 1914.

Carry on down Marylebone Lane, crossing over Bulstrode Street and Bentinck St/Hinde Street.

Continue down Marylebone Lane, crossing over Wigmore Street.
On the left is Steinway Hall, the London showroom and rehearsal rooms for Steinway & Sons' pianos. Opened in 1875, the hall was the first Steinway showroom in Europe (their head office being in New York City).

The road forks at the Radisson Edwardian Hotel. Take either fork to Oxford Street.

Turn right onto Oxford Street and walk past Stratford Place on your right.
This area was once the site of a great water conduit that supplied neighbouring properties with fresh water from the River Tyburn. A bridge spanned the river near the junction with Oxford Street.

After passing Stratford Place, turn left into Davies Street.
Here the road forks – the left-hand fork is South Molton Street, home to numerous upmarket boutiques. In the middle of the fork is a narrow art deco building (previously The Hog in the Pound pub).

Walk a short distance down Davies Street to Gray's Antiques Market – a tall redbrick building.
Gray's was originally the Grosvenor Works of Bolding & Sons – manufacturers of sanitary fittings and equipment. The firm was founded in 1822 in nearby South Molton Street and went on to become one of the 19th century's premier manufacturers of bathroom fittings. Although the firm closed in the late 1960s, their toilets, sinks and basins are still in great demand and Victorian pieces in good condition sell for far more money today than they did when new. Bolding's factory was purchased by Bennie Gray in 1977 and shortly afterwards reopened

as Gray's Antiques Market – an eclectic mix of independent antique dealers specialising in all manner of products, from jewellery to ceramics. Gray's is open from 10am-6pm Monday to Friday and 11am-5pm Saturday.

Walk down the left-hand side of Gray's and into Davies Mews on your right, where you will find the Gray's Mews Market. Go into the market and down the staircase in the centre of the building.
When Bennie Gray bought the Bolding factory, he found that the basement of the mews was flooded with several feet of water. Engineers were sent to investigate where the water was coming from and made the amazing discovery that the source was actually an ancient spring from the River Tyburn. Gray decided to turn the spring into a feature and enclosed it in a decorative channel complete with fish, which runs the length of the basement. Today, Gray's Mews is the only place in the West End where the waters of the Tyburn can still be seen.

Once you have finished browsing the antique stalls, come out of Gray's Mews and turn right up Davies Mews. At the top, turn left back into Davies Street.

Cross over Brook Street (named after the Tyburn) and carry on down past Claridge's Hotel (on your left).

Cross over Grosvenor Street and past Alfred Dunhill.
Otherwise known as Bourdon House, the Alfred Dunhill building is one of the oldest private properties in Mayfair. The original part of the house was built in the 1720s for William Bourdon, a local Justice of the Peace and vestryman of St George's, Hanover Square. Although the building was greatly enlarged over the ensuing centuries, the exterior retains much of its Georgian character and provides some architectural interest in an otherwise rather bland stretch of Davies Street.

Carry on down Davies Street until you get to Berkeley Square. Cross over the road and walk through the square.
Berkeley Square was laid out in the 1730s on land owned by Lord Berkeley of Stratton, who lived nearby on Piccadilly. The development was an instant success and the houses surrounding the square quickly filled with wealthy and influential tenants, including the Earl of Bute (who lived in Lansdowne House) and Horace

Walpole. The gazebo in the centre of the Square was built in the 1820s as a pump house, where visitors could take the famed waters of the Tyburn.

When you reach the other side of Berkeley Square, turn right and then left into Fitzmaurice Place.

Continue down Fitzmaurice Place and follow the road around to your right into Curzon Street.
Curzon Street is named after its developer Sir Nathaniel Curzon, who laid out the street *circa* 1710. The land it occupied had previously been the site of the annual May fair, which inadvertently gave the area the name by which it remains known.

When you reach the impressive Third Church of Christ the Scientist, turn left down Half Moon Street.

At the bottom of Half Moon Street, cross over Piccadilly and into Green Park.
Originally a royal hunting park created by Charles II in 1668, Green Park is one of the city's great open spaces. However, back in the 18th century the park was a notorious resort of highwaymen and footpads, who made a good living from robbing wealthy passers-by, including Berkeley Square resident Horace Walpole.

Walk straight down the main path through the park to Canada Gate.
This elaborate entranceway, which forms part of the Victoria Memorial, was installed in 1908 to commemorate Canada's contribution to the British Empire.

Turn right and cross the road to Buckingham Palace.
Here the Tyburn forms a delta and splits in two again. The southern branch runs down Palace Street and across Victoria Street into Vauxhall Bridge Road. It then flows under Tachbrook Street before entering the Thames near Crown Reach. Our route follows the eastern branch.

Walk past the front of the palace; when you reach the other side of the building, cross over the road and turn right. You will exit the palace grounds through a black iron gate flanked by white stone columns. Once out of the gate, turn left down Buckingham Gate.

Walk past the Guards' Museum (open 10-4 daily) and continue down Buckingham Gate.
The unusual building with the ship mounted above its ground floor is the Swaziland High Commission.

Turn left into Petty France.
This ancient street was first recorded in 1494. Its name, 'Little France', was probably derived from the number of French merchants living in the area in medieval times.

Continue down Petty France, past the Wellington Barracks and St James's Park Tube station.
This station forms part of a huge office block known as 55 Broadway, built between 1927-29 as the headquarters for London Underground's predecessor, the Underground Electric Railways Company of London (UERL). The station's booking hall (which includes the main entrance into the upstairs offices) is a great example of a commercial art deco interior. Outside, an important pair of Epstein sculptures, entitled *Day* and *Night*, grace the north and east façades.

Continue straight into Tothill Street, past the Methodist Central Hall on your left, then cross over the road to the entrance of Westminster Abbey.
Here, the Tyburn splits once again. One fork travels underground across Parliament Square and up Parliament Street before reaching the Thames at the former Scotland Yard. The other branch heads south down Great Smith Street, across Smith Square to the Thames near Lambeth Bridge. These two branches of the river originally formed the watery boundary of Thorney Island – an ancient sacred place, inextricably linked with Christianity since the seventh century AD. The current abbey, inaugurated by Edward the Confessor in the 11th century, has witnessed London's evolution. It has stood through riots, plague and war, remaining a citadel at the heart of this great city. It is worth staying awhile outside the Abbey to imagine how the landscape that surrounds it has changed as the centuries have passed.

We now trace the final stage of the Tyburn's journey to the Thames. Walk down past Westminster Abbey towards the Houses of Parliament. Turn right into St Margaret Street, cross the road and enter Victoria Tower Gardens. Walk to the edge of the gardens and look over the wall to the Thames.

Here, the Tyburn's course from the hills of Hampstead ends. We have ended our journey too. Take a well-earned rest in the gardens before heading back past the Houses of Parliament, along the south side of Parliament Square. A short way up Bridge Street, on your right, you will find Westminster Underground station (District, Circle and Jubilee Lines).

SELECT BIBLIOGRAPHY

Ackroyd, P. *London: The Biography* (2001) Vintage

Bacon, G. W. *The A to Z of Victorian London* (1987) London Topographical Society

Beavan, A. H. *Up-To-Date Locomotion* (1903) G. Routledge & Sons

Booth, C. *Descriptive Map of London Poverty* (1984) London Topographical Society

Brandon-Thomas, J. *Passing Brompton Road: A Play in Three Acts* (1922)

Connor, J. E. *Abandoned Stations on London's Underground* (2000) Connor & Butler

Day, J. R. and Reed, J. *The Story of London's Underground* (2010) Capital Transport

De Amicis, E. *Jottings about London* (1883) Alfred Mudge & Son

Dickens, C. Jnr. *Dickens's Dictionary of London 1888* (1995) Old House Books

Gavin, H. *Sanitary Ramblings: 1848* (1971) Frank Cass Publishers

Gilbert, M. *The Second World War* (2009) Phoenix

Godwin, G. *Town Swamps and Social Bridges* (1859) Routledge Warne & Routledge

Greenwood, J. *Unsentimental Journeys (1867)* (2009) Dodo Press

Halliday, S. *The Great Stink of London* (2001) The History Press

Harris, C. M. *What's in a Name?* (2001) Capital Transport

Hobhouse, H. (ed.) *Survey of London* (1994) English Heritage

Hollingshead, J. *Ragged London in 1861* (1861) Smith, Elder & Co

Johnson, S. *The Ghost Map* (2007) Riverhead Books

Keegan, J. *The First World War* (1999) Pimlico

Keegan, J. *The Second World War* (1997) Pimlico

Lecount, P. *A Practical Treatise on Railways* (1839) A. & C. Black

Mayhew, H. *London Labour and the London Poor* (1965) Oxford University Press

Pearsall, P. *London A-Z Street Atlas* (1937) Geographers' Map Company

Roque, J. *A to Z of Georgian London* (1982) London Topographical Society
Smith, S. *Underground London* (2005) Abacus
Stevenson, D. *1914-1918: The History of the First World War* (2005) Penguin
Stow, J. *A Survey of London: 1598* (2005) The History Press
Thornbury, W. *Old and New London* (1897) Cassell
Trench, R. and Hillman, E. *London under London* (1993) John Murray
Welbourn, N. *Lost Lines* (2004) Ian Allan Publishing
White, J. *London in the 19th Century* (2007) Jonathan Cape
Whitfield, P. *London: A Life in Maps* (2006) British Library
Who's Who?
Williams, F. S. *Our Iron Roads* (1888) R. Bentley & Son
Wolmar, C. *The Subterranean Railway* (2005) Atlantic Books

Selected Online Resources
1911 Census
1911 Encyclopaedia
Access to Archives
Ancestry
British Newspaper Archive
Charles Booth Online
Dictionary of Victorian London
Family Search
Free BMD
Genuki
Google Maps
Old Bailey Online
Old Maps
Old London Maps
Oxford Dictionary of National Biography
Victoria County History
Westminster Libraries

Newspaper Archives
Blackwood's Magazine
Burlington Magazine
Daily Express
Daily Mirror

The Economist
Financial Times
The Gentleman's Magazine
The Guardian
Illustrated London News
The Observer
Picture Post
Punch
Sunday Express
Sunday Times
The Times

INDEX

ひ